RESUMES FOR

SALES AND MARKETING CAREERS

THIRD EDITION

RESUMES FOR

SALES AND MARKETING CAREERS

With Sample Cover Letters

The Editors of McGraw-Hill

McGraw-Hill

New York   Chicago   San Francisco   Lisbon   London   Madrid   Mexico City
Milan   New Delhi   San Juan   Seoul   Singapore   Sydney   Toronto

The **McGraw·Hill** Companies

Library of Congress Cataloging-in-Publication Data

Resumes for sales and marketing careers : with sample cover letters / the editors of
McGraw-Hill.—3rd ed.
     p.   cm. — (McGraw-Hill professional resumes series)
   ISBN 0-07-143851-3 (pbk. : alk. paper)
   1. Resumes (Employment)   2. Sales personnel.   3. Marketing.   I. Series.

HF5383.R45   2005
650.14'2—dc22   2004059290

2 3 4 5 6 7 8 9 0   VLP/VLP   0 9 8 7 6 5

ISBN 0-07-143851-3

McGraw-Hill books are available at special quantity discounts to use as premiums and sales
promotions, or for use in corporate training programs. For more information, please write to
the Director of Special Sales, Professional Publishing, McGraw-Hill, Two Penn Plaza, New
York, NY 10121-2298. Or contact your local bookstore.

This book is printed on acid-free paper.

Contents

Introduction

Your resume is a piece of paper (or an electronic document) that serves to introduce you to the people who will eventually hire you. To write a thoughtful resume, you must thoroughly assess your personality, your accomplishments, and the skills you have acquired. The act of composing and submitting a resume also requires you to carefully consider the company or individual that might hire you. What are they looking for, and how can you meet their needs? This book shows you how to organize your personal information and experience into a concise and well-written resume so that your qualifications and potential as an employee will be understood easily and quickly by a complete stranger.

Writing the resume is just one step in what can be a daunting job-search process, but it is an important element in the chain of events that will lead you to your new position. While you are probably a talented, bright, and charming person, your resume may not reflect these qualities. A poorly written resume can get you nowhere; a well-written resume can land you an interview and potentially a job. A good resume can even lead the interviewer to ask you questions that will allow you to talk about your strengths and highlight the skills you can bring to a prospective employer. Even a person with very little experience can find a good job if he or she is assisted by a thoughtful and polished resume.

Lengthy, typewritten resumes are a thing of the past. Today, employers do not have the time or the patience for verbose documents; they look for tightly composed, straightforward, action-based resumes. Although a one-page resume is the norm, a two-page resume may be warranted if you have had extensive job experience or have changed careers and truly need the space to properly position yourself. If, after careful editing, you still need more than one page to present yourself, it's acceptable to use a second page. A crowded resume that's hard to read would be the worst of your choices.

Distilling your work experience, education, and interests into such a small space requires preparation and thought. This book takes you step-by-step through the process of crafting an effective resume that will stand out in today's competitive marketplace. It serves as a workbook and a place to write down your experiences, while also including the techniques you'll need to pull all the necessary elements together. In the following pages, you'll find many examples of resumes that are specific to your area of interest. Study them for inspiration and find what appeals to you. There are a variety of ways to organize and present your information; inside, you'll find several that will be suitable to your needs. Good luck landing the job of your dreams!

RESUMES FOR

SALES AND MARKETING CAREERS

The Elements of an Effective Resume

An effective resume is composed of information that employers are most interested in knowing about a prospective job applicant. This information is conveyed by a few essential elements. The following is a list of elements that are found in most resumes—some essential, some optional. Later in this chapter, we will further examine the role of each of these elements in the makeup of your resume.

- Heading

- Objective and/or Keyword Section

- Work Experience

- Education

- Honors

- Activities

- Certificates and Licenses

- Publications

- Professional Memberships

- Special Skills

- Personal Information

- References

The first step in preparing your resume is to gather information about yourself and your past accomplishments. Later you will refine this information, rewrite it using effective language, and organize it into an attractive layout. But first, let's take a look at each of these important elements individually so you can judge their appropriateness for your resume.

Heading

Although the heading may seem to be the simplest section of your resume, be careful not to take it lightly. It is the first section your prospective employer will see, and it contains the information she or he will need to contact you. At the very least, the heading must contain your name, your home address, and, of course, a phone number where you can be reached easily.

In today's high-tech world, many of us have multiple ways that we can be contacted. You may list your e-mail address if you are reasonably sure the employer makes use of this form of communication. Keep in mind, however, that others may have access to your e-mail messages if you send them from an account provided by your current company. If this is a concern, do not list your work e-mail address on your resume. If you are able to take calls at your current place of business, you should include your work number, because most employers will attempt to contact you during typical business hours.

If you have voice mail or a reliable answering machine at home or at work, list its number in the heading and make sure your greeting is professional and clear. Always include at least one phone number in your heading, even if it is a temporary number, where a prospective employer can leave a message.

You might have a dozen different ways to be contacted, but you do not need to list all of them. Confine your numbers or addresses to those that are the easiest for the prospective employer to use and the simplest for you to retrieve.

Objective

When seeking a specific career path, it is important to list a job or career objective on your resume. This statement helps employers know the direction you see yourself taking, so they can determine whether your goals are in line with those of their organization and the position available. Normally, an objective is one to two sentences long. Its contents will vary depending on your career field, goals, and personality. The objective can be specific or general, but it should always be to the point. See the sample resumes in this book for examples.

If you are planning to use this resume online, or you suspect your potential employer is likely to scan your resume, you will want to include a "keyword" in the objective. This allows a prospective employer, searching hundreds of resumes for a specific skill or position objective, to locate the keyword and find your resume. In essence, a keyword is what's "hot" in your particular field at a given time. It's a buzzword, a shorthand way of getting a particular message across at a glance. For example, if you are a lawyer, your objective might state your desire to work in the area of corporate litigation. In this case, someone searching for the keyword "corporate litigation" will pull up your resume and know that you want to plan, research, and present cases at trial on behalf of the corporation. If your objective states that you "desire a challenging position in systems design," the keyword is "systems design," an industry-specific shorthand way of saying that you want to be involved in assessing the need for, acquiring, and implementing high-technology systems. These are keywords and every industry has them, so it's becoming more and more important to include a few in your resume. (You may need to conduct additional research to make sure you know what keywords are most likely to be used in your desired industry, profession, or situation.)

There are many resume and job-search sites online. Like most things in the online world, they vary a great deal in quality. Use your discretion. If you plan to apply for jobs online or advertise your availability this way, you will want to design a scannable resume. This type of resume uses a format that can be easily scanned into a computer and added to a database. Scanning allows a prospective employer to use keywords to quickly review each applicant's experience and skills, and (in the event that there are many candidates for the job) to keep your resume for future reference.

Many people find that it is worthwhile to create two or more versions of their basic resume. You may want an intricately designed resume on high-quality paper to mail or hand out *and* a resume that is designed to be scanned into a computer and saved on a database or an online job site. You can even create a resume in ASCII text to e-mail to prospective employers. For further information, you may wish to refer to the *Guide to Internet Job Searching*, by Frances Roehm and Margaret Dikel, updated and published every other year by McGraw-Hill. This excellent book contains helpful and detailed information about formatting a resume for Internet use. To get you started, in Chapter 3 we have included a list of things to keep in mind when creating electronic resumes.

Although it is usually a good idea to include an objective, in some cases this element is not necessary. The goal of the objective statement is to provide the employer with an idea of where you see yourself going in the field. However, if you are uncertain of the exact nature of the job you seek, including an objective that is too specific could result in your not being considered for a host of perfectly acceptable positions. If you decide not to use an objective heading in your resume, you should definitely incorporate the information that would be conveyed in the objective into your cover letter.

Work Experience

Work experience is arguably the most important element of them all. Unless you are a recent graduate or former homemaker with little or no relevant work experience, your current and former positions will provide the central focus of the resume. You will want this section to be as complete and carefully constructed as possible. By thoroughly examining your work experience, you can get to the heart of your accomplishments and present them in a way that demonstrates and highlights your qualifications.

If you are just entering the workforce, your resume will probably focus on your education, but you should also include information on your work or volunteer experiences. Although you will have less information about work experience than a person who has held multiple positions or is advanced in his or her career, the amount of information is not what is most important in this section. How the information is presented and what it says about you as a worker and a person are what really count.

As you create this section of your resume, remember the need for accuracy. Include all the necessary information about each of your jobs, including your job title, dates of employment, name of your employer, city, state, responsibilities, special projects you handled, and accomplishments. Be sure to list only accomplishments for which you were directly responsible. And don't be alarmed if you haven't participated in or worked on special projects, because this section may not be relevant to certain jobs.

The most common way to list your work experience is in *reverse chronological order*. In other words, start with your most recent job and work your way backward. This way, your prospective employer sees your current (and often most important) position before considering your past employment. Your most recent position, if it's the most important in terms of responsibilities and relevance to the job for which you are applying, should also be the one that includes the most information as compared to your previous positions.

Even if the work itself seems unrelated to your proposed career path, you should list any job or experience that will help sell your talents. If you were promoted or given greater responsibilities or commendations, be sure to mention the fact.

The following worksheet is provided to help you organize your experiences in the working world. It will also serve as an excellent resource to refer to when updating your resume in the future.

WORK EXPERIENCE

Job One:

Job Title _____

Dates _____

Employer _____

City, State _____

Major Duties _____

_____

_____

_____

_____

_____

_____

_____

Special Projects _____

_____

_____

Accomplishments _____

_____

_____

_____

_____

Job Four:

Job Title _____

Dates _____

Employer _____

City, State _____

Major Duties _____

_____

_____

_____

_____

_____

_____

_____

Special Projects _____

_____

_____

_____

Accomplishments _____

_____

_____

_____

_____

_____

_____

_____

Education

Education is usually the second most important element of a resume. Your educational background is often a deciding factor in an employer's decision to interview you. Highlight your accomplishments in school as much as you did those accomplishments at work. If you are looking for your first professional job, your education or life experience will be your greatest asset because your related work experience will be minimal. In this case, the education section becomes the most important means of selling yourself.

Include in this section all the degrees or certificates you have received; your major or area of concentration; all of the honors you earned; and any relevant activities you participated in, organized, or chaired. Again, list your most recent schooling first. If you have completed graduate-level work, begin with that and work your way back through your undergraduate education. If you have completed college, you generally should not list your high-school experience; do so only if you earned special honors, you had a grade point average that was much better than the norm, or this was your highest level of education.

If you have completed a large number of credit hours in a subject that may be relevant to the position you are seeking but did not obtain a degree, you may wish to list the hours or classes you completed. Keep in mind, however, that you may be asked to explain why you did not finish the program. If you are currently in school, list the degree, certificate, or license you expect to obtain and the projected date of completion.

The following worksheet will help you gather the information you need for this section of your resume.

EDUCATION

School One _____

Major or Area of Concentration _____

Degree _____

Dates _____

School Two _____

Major or Area of Concentration _____

Degree _____

Dates _____

Honors

If you include an honors section in your resume, you should highlight any awards, honors, or memberships in honorary societies that you have received. (You may also incorporate this information into your education section.) Often, the honors are academic in nature, but this section also may be used for special achievements in sports, clubs, or other school activities. Always include the name of the organization awarding the honor and the date(s) received. Use the following worksheet to help you gather your information.

HONORS

Honor One _____

Awarding Organization _____

Date(s) _____

Honor Two _____

Awarding Organization _____

Date(s) _____

Honor Three _____

Awarding Organization _____

Date(s) _____

Honor Four _____

Awarding Organization _____

Date(s) _____

Honor Five _____

Awarding Organization _____

Date(s) _____

Activities

Perhaps you have been active in different organizations or clubs; often an employer will look at such involvement as evidence of initiative, dedication, and good social skills. Examples of your ability to take a leading role in a group should be included on a resume, if you can provide them. The activities section of your resume should present neighborhood and community activities, volunteer positions, and so forth. In general, you may want to avoid listing any organization whose name indicates the race, creed, sex, age, marital status, sexual orientation, or nation of origin of its members because this could expose you to discrimination. Use the following worksheet to list the specifics of your activities.

ACTIVITIES

Organization/Activity _____

Accomplishments _____

_____

_____

Organization/Activity _____

Accomplishments _____

_____

_____

Organization/Activity _____

Accomplishments _____

_____

_____

As your work experience grows through the years, your school activities and honors will carry less weight and be emphasized less in your resume. Eventually, you will probably list only your degree and any major honors received. As time goes by, your job performance and the experience you've gained become the most important elements in your resume, which should change to reflect this.

Certificates and Licenses

If your chosen career path requires specialized training, you may already have certificates or licenses. You should list these if the job you are seeking requires them and you, of course, have acquired them. If you have applied for a license but have not yet received it, use the phrase "application pending."

License requirements vary by state. If you have moved or are planning to relocate to another state, check with that state's board or licensing agency for all licensing requirements.

Always make sure that all of the information you list is completely accurate. Locate copies of your certificates and licenses, and check the exact date and name of the accrediting agency. Use the following worksheet to organize the necessary information.

CERTIFICATES AND LICENSES

Name of License _____

Licensing Agency _____

Date Issued _____

Name of License _____

Licensing Agency _____

Date Issued _____

Name of License _____

Licensing Agency _____

Date Issued _____

Publications

Some professions strongly encourage or even require that you publish. If you have written, coauthored, or edited any books, articles, professional papers, or works of a similar nature that pertain to your field, you will definitely want to include this element. Remember to list the date of publication and the publisher's name, and specify whether you were the sole author or a coauthor. Book, magazine, or journal titles are generally italicized, while the titles of articles within a larger publication appear in quotes. (Check with your reference librarian for more about the appropriate way to present this information.) For scientific or research papers, you will need to give the date, place, and audience to whom the paper was presented.

Use the following worksheet to help you gather the necessary information about your publications.

PUBLICATIONS

Title and Type (Note, Article, etc.) _____

Title of Publication (Journal, Book, etc.) _____

Publisher _____

Date Published _____

Title and Type (Note, Article, etc.) _____

Title of Publication (Journal, Book, etc.) _____

Publisher _____

Date Published _____

Title and Type (Note, Article, etc.) _____

Title of Publication (Journal, Book, etc.) _____

Publisher _____

Date Published _____

Professional Memberships

Another potential element in your resume is a section listing professional memberships. Use this section to describe your involvement in professional associations, unions, and similar organizations. It is to your advantage to list any professional memberships that pertain to the job you are seeking. Many employers see your membership as representative of your desire to stay up-to-date and connected in your field. Include the dates of your involvement and whether you took part in any special activities or held any offices within the organization. Use the following worksheet to organize your information.

PROFESSIONAL MEMBERSHIPS

Name of Organization _____

Office(s) Held_____

Activities _____

Dates _____

Name of Organization _____

Office(s) Held_____

Activities _____

Dates _____

Name of Organization _____

Office(s) Held_____

Activities _____

Dates _____

Name of Organization _____

Office(s) Held_____

Activities _____

Dates _____

Special Skills

The special skills section of your resume is the place to mention any special abilities you have that relate to the job you are seeking. You can use this element to present certain talents or experiences that are not necessarily a part of your education or work experience. Common examples include fluency in a foreign language, extensive travel abroad, or knowledge of a particular computer application. "Special skills" can encompass a wide range of talents, and this section can be used creatively. However, for each skill you list, you should be able to describe how it would be a direct asset in the type of work you're seeking because employers may ask just that in an interview. If you can't think of a way to do this, it may be extraneous information.

Personal Information

Some people include personal information on their resumes. This is generally not recommended, but you might wish to include it if you think that something in your personal life, such as a hobby or talent, has some bearing on the position you are seeking. This type of information is often referred to at the beginning of an interview, when it may be used as an icebreaker. Of course, personal information regarding your age, marital status, race, religion, or sexual orientation should never appear on your resume as personal information. It should be given only in the context of memberships and activities, and only when doing so would not expose you to discrimination.

References

References are not usually given on the resume itself, but a prospective employer needs to know that you have references who may be contacted if necessary. All you need to include is a single sentence at the end of the resume: "References are available upon request," or even simply, "References available." Have a reference list ready—your interviewer may ask to see it! Contact each person on the list ahead of time to see whether it is all right for you to use him or her as a reference. This way, the person has a chance to think about what to say *before* the call occurs. This helps ensure that you will obtain the best reference possible.

Chapter 2

Writing Your Resume

Now that you have gathered the information for each section of your resume, it's time to write it out in a way that will get the attention of the reviewer—hopefully, your future employer! The language you use in your resume will affect its success, so you must be careful and conscientious. Translate the facts you have gathered into the active, precise language of resume writing. You will be aiming for a resume that keeps the reader's interest and highlights your accomplishments in a concise and effective way.

Resume writing is unlike any other form of writing. Although your seventh-grade composition teacher would not approve, the rules of punctuation and sentence building are often completely ignored. Instead, you should try for a functional, direct writing style that focuses on the use of verbs and other words that imply action on your part. Writing with action words and strong verbs characterizes you to potential employers as an energetic, active person, someone who completes tasks and achieves results from his or her work. Resumes that do not make use of action words can sound passive and stale. These resumes are not effective and do not get the attention of any employer, no matter how qualified the applicant. Choose words that display your strengths and demonstrate your initiative. The following list of commonly used verbs will help you create a strong resume:

administered	assembled
advised	assumed responsibility
analyzed	billed
arranged	built

carried out	inspected
channeled	interviewed
collected	introduced
communicated	invented
compiled	maintained
completed	managed
conducted	met with
contacted	motivated
contracted	negotiated
coordinated	operated
counseled	orchestrated
created	ordered
cut	organized
designed	oversaw
determined	performed
developed	planned
directed	prepared
dispatched	presented
distributed	produced
documented	programmed
edited	published
established	purchased
expanded	recommended
functioned as	recorded
gathered	reduced
handled	referred
hired	represented
implemented	researched
improved	reviewed

saved	supervised
screened	taught
served as	tested
served on	trained
sold	typed
suggested	wrote

Let's look at two examples that differ only in their writing style. The first resume section is ineffective because it does not use action words to accent the applicant's work experiences.

WORK EXPERIENCE
Regional Sales Manager

Manager of sales representatives from seven states. Manager of twelve food chain accounts in the East. In charge of the sales force's planned selling toward specific goals. Supervisor and trainer of new sales representatives. Consulting for customers in the areas of inventory management and quality control.

Special Projects: Coordinator and sponsor of annual Food Industry Seminar.

Accomplishments: Monthly regional volume went up 25 percent during my tenure while, at the same time, a proper sales/cost ratio was maintained. Customer-company relations were improved.

In the following paragraph, we have rewritten the same section using action words. Notice how the tone has changed. It now sounds stronger and more active. This person accomplished goals and really *did* things.

WORK EXPERIENCE
Regional Sales Manager

Managed sales representatives from seven states. Oversaw twelve food chain accounts in the eastern United States. Directed the sales force in planned selling toward specific goals. Supervised and trained new sales representatives. Counseled customers in the areas of inventory management and quality control. Coordinated and sponsored the annual Food Industry Seminar. Increased monthly regional volume by 25 percent and helped to improve customer-company relations during my tenure.

One helpful way to construct the work experience section is to make use of your actual job descriptions—the written duties and expectations your employers have for a person in your current or former position. Job descriptions are rarely written in proper resume language, so you will have to rework them, but they do include much of the information necessary to create this section of your resume. If you have access to job descriptions for your former positions, you can use the details to construct an action-oriented paragraph. Often, your human resources department can provide a job description for your current position.

The following is an example of a typical human resources job description, followed by a rewritten version of the same description employing action words and specific details about the job. Again, pay attention to the style of writing instead of the content, as the details of your own experience will be unique.

WORK EXPERIENCE
Public Administrator I

Responsibilities: Coordinate and direct public services to meet the needs of the nation, state, or community. Analyze problems; work with special committees and public agencies; recommend solutions to governing bodies.

Aptitudes and Skills: Ability to relate to and communicate with people; solve complex problems through analysis; plan, organize, and implement policies and programs. Knowledge of political systems, financial management, personnel administration, program evaluation, and organizational theory.

WORK EXPERIENCE
Public Administrator I

Wrote pamphlets and conducted discussion groups to inform citizens of legislative processes and consumer issues. Organized and supervised 25 interviewers. Trained interviewers in effective communication skills.

After you have written out your resume, you are ready to begin the next important step: assembly and layout.

Chapter 3

Assembly and Layout

At this point, you've gathered all the necessary information for your resume and rewritten it in language that will impress your potential employers. Your next step is to assemble the sections in a logical order and lay them out on the page neatly and attractively to achieve the desired effect: getting the interview.

Assembly

The order of the elements in a resume makes a difference in its overall effect. Clearly, you would not want to bury your name and address somewhere in the middle of the resume. Nor would you want to lead with a less important section, such as special skills. Put the elements in an order that stresses your most important accomplishments and the things that will be most appealing to your potential employer. For example, if you are new to the workforce, you will want the reviewer to read about your education and life skills before any part-time jobs you may have held for short durations. On the other hand, if you have been gainfully employed for several years and currently hold an important position in your company, you should list your work accomplishments ahead of your educational information, which has become less pertinent with time.

Certain things should always be included in your resume, but others are optional. The following list shows you which are which. You might want to use it as a checklist to be certain that you have included all of the necessary information.

Essential	Optional
Name	Cellular Phone Number
Address	Pager Number
Phone Number	E-Mail Address or Website Address
Work Experience	Voice Mail Number
Education	Job Objective
References Phrase	Honors
	Special Skills
	Publications
	Professional Memberships
	Activities
	Certificates and Licenses
	Personal Information
	Graphics
	Photograph

Your choice of optional sections depends on your own background and employment needs. Always use information that will put you in a favorable light—unless it's absolutely essential, avoid anything that will prompt the interviewer to ask questions about your weaknesses or something else that could be unflattering. Make sure your information is accurate and truthful. If your honors are impressive, include them in the resume. If your activities in school demonstrate talents that are necessary for the job you are seeking, allow space for a section on activities. If you are applying for a position that requires ornamental illustration, you may want to include border illustrations or graphics that demonstrate your talents in this area. If you are answering an advertisement for a job that requires certain physical traits, a photo of yourself might be appropriate. A person applying for a job as a computer programmer would *not* include a photo as part of his or her resume. Each resume is unique, just as each person is unique.

Types of Resumes

So far we have focused on the most common type of resume—the *reverse chronological* resume—in which your most recent job is listed first. This is the type of resume usually preferred by those who have to read a large number of resumes, and it is by far the most popular and widely circulated. However, this style of presentation may not be the most effective way to highlight *your* skills and accomplishments.

For example, if you are reentering the workforce after many years or are trying to change career fields, the *functional* resume may work best. This type of resume puts the focus on your achievements instead of the sequence of your work history. In the functional resume, your experience is presented through your general accomplishments and the skills you have developed in your working life.

A functional resume is assembled from the same information you gathered in Chapter 1. The main difference lies in how you organize the information. Essentially, the work experience section is divided in two, with your job duties and accomplishments constituting one section and your employers' names, cities, and states; your positions; and the dates employed making up the other. Place the first section near the top of your resume, just below your job objective (if used), and call it *Accomplishments* or *Achievements*. The second section, containing the bare essentials of your work history, should come after the accomplishments section and can be called *Employment History*, since it is a chronological overview of your former jobs.

The other sections of your resume remain the same. The work experience section is the only one affected in the functional format. By placing the section that focuses on your achievements at the beginning, you draw attention to these achievements. This puts less emphasis on where you worked and when, and more on what you did and what you are capable of doing.

If you are changing careers, the emphasis on skills and achievements is important. The identities of previous employers (who aren't part of your new career field) need to be downplayed. A functional resume can help accomplish this task. If you are reentering the workforce after a long absence, a functional resume is the obvious choice. And if you lack full-time work experience, you will need to draw attention away from this fact and put the focus on your skills and abilities. You may need to highlight your volunteer activities and part-time work. Education may also play a more important role in your resume.

The type of resume that is right for you will depend on your personal circumstances. It may be helpful to create both types and then compare them. Which one presents you in the best light? Examples of both types of resumes are included in this book. Use the sample resumes in Chapter 5 to help you decide on the content, presentation, and look of your own resume.

Resume or Curriculum Vitae?

A curriculum vitae (CV) is a longer, more detailed synopsis of your professional history, which generally runs three or more pages in length. It includes a summary of your educational and academic background as well as teaching and research experience, publications, presentations, awards, honors, affiliations, and other details. Because the purpose of the CV is different from that of the resume, many of the rules we've discussed thus far involving style and length do not apply.

A curriculum vitae is used primarily for admissions applications to graduate or professional schools, independent consulting in a variety of settings, proposals for fellowships or grants, or applications for positions in academia. As with a resume, you may need different versions of a CV for different types of positions. You should only send a CV when one is specifically requested by an employer or institution.

Like a resume, your CV should include your name, contact information, education, skills, and experience. In addition to the basics, a CV includes research and teaching experience, publications, grants and fellowships, professional associations and licenses, awards, and other information relevant to the position for which you are applying. You can follow the advice presented thus far to gather and organize your personal information.

Special Tips for Electronic Resumes

Because there are many details to consider in writing a resume that will be posted or transmitted on the Internet, or one that will be scanned into a computer when it is received, we suggest that you refer to the *Guide to Internet Job Searching*, by Frances Roehm and Margaret Dikel, as previously mentioned. However, here are some brief, general guidelines to follow if you expect your resume to be scanned into a computer.

- Use standard fonts in which none of the letters touch.

- Keep in mind that underlining, italics, and fancy scripts may not scan well.

- Use boldface and capitalization to set off elements. Again, make sure letters don't touch. Leave at least a quarter inch between lines of type.

- Keep information and elements at the left margin. Centering, columns, and even indenting may change when the resume is optically scanned.

- Do not use any lines, boxes, or graphics.

- Place the most important information at the top of the first page. If you use two pages, put "Page 1 of 2" at the bottom of the first page and put your name and "Page 2 of 2" at the top of the second page.

- List each telephone number on its own line in the header.

- Use multiple keywords or synonyms for what you do to make sure your qualifications will be picked up if a prospective employer is searching for them. Use nouns that are keywords for your profession.

- Be descriptive in your titles. For example, don't just use "assistant"; use "legal office assistant."

- Make sure the contrast between print and paper is good. Use a high-quality laser printer and white or very light colored 8½-by-11-inch paper.

- Mail a high-quality laser print or an excellent copy. Do not fold or use staples, as this might interfere with scanning. You may, however, use paper clips.

In addition to creating a resume that works well for scanning, you may want to have a resume that can be e-mailed to reviewers. Because you may not know what word processing application the recipient uses, the best format to use is ASCII text. (ASCII stands for "American Standard Code for Information Interchange.") It allows people with very different software platforms to exchange and understand information. (E-mail operates on this principle.) ASCII is a simple, text-only language, which means you can include only simple text. There can be no use of boldface, italics, or even paragraph indentations.

To create an ASCII resume, just use your normal word processing program; when finished, save it as a "text only" document. You will find this option under the "save" or "save as" command. Here is a list of things to *avoid* when crafting your electronic resume:

- Tabs. Use your space bar. Tabs will not work.

- Any special characters, such as mathematical symbols.

- Word wrap. Use hard returns (the return key) to make line breaks.

- Centering or other formatting. Align everything at the left margin.

- Bold or italic fonts. Everything will be converted to plain text when you save the file as a "text only" document.

Check carefully for any mistakes before you save the document as a text file. Spellcheck and proofread it several times; then ask someone with a keen eye to go over it again for you. Remember: the key is to keep it simple. Any attempt to make this resume pretty or decorative may result in a resume that is confusing and hard to read. After you have saved the document, you can cut and paste it into an e-mail or onto a website.

Layout for a Paper Resume

A great deal of care—and much more formatting—is necessary to achieve an attractive layout for your paper resume. There is no single appropriate layout that applies to every resume, but there are a few basic rules to follow in putting your resume on paper:

- Leave a comfortable margin on the sides, top, and bottom of the page (usually one to one and a half inches).

- Use appropriate spacing between the sections (two to three line spaces are usually adequate).

- Be consistent in the *type* of headings you use for different sections of your resume. For example, if you capitalize the heading EMPLOY-MENT HISTORY, don't use initial capitals and underlining for a section of equal importance, such as Education.

- Do not use more than one font in your resume. Stay consistent by choosing a font that is fairly standard and easy to read, and don't change it for different sections. Beware of the tendency to try to make your resume original by choosing fancy type styles; your resume may end up looking unprofessional instead of creative. Unless you are in a very creative and artistic field, you should almost always stick with tried-and-true type styles like Times New Roman and Palatino, which are often used in business writing. In the area of resume styles, conservative is usually the best way to go.

CHRONOLOGICAL RESUME

Darien Phillips

4699 Franklin Street • Royal Oak, MI 48066
D.Phillips@xxx.com • (810) 555-1889

OBJECTIVE

Seeking management position in marketing with a major financial publication.

WORK HISTORY

Time Inc. - *Money* Magazine, Midwest Sales Assistant, 3/02–Present
- Plan & execute all special events
- Develop, write, edit, & design two newsletters: *TIME INK* & *Cairns' Corner*
- Maintain monthly expenses & yearly budgets
- Communicate directly with client & agency personnel regarding all aspects of the publications
- Develop marketing & sales tools to heighten awareness of Time Inc.'s Personal Finance Group

Wayne State University, Campaign Gift Tracking Assistant, 3/00–3/02
- Ensured accuracy of gifts & pledges of $25,000 or more in accounting system
- Verified & maintained files on all large donors & trustees for reference for both development & accounting staff
- Generated weekly financial reports regarding over $900 million to be dispersed university-wide

U.S. Department of Agriculture, Internship, Editorial Asst./Office Mgr., 5/98–12/99
- Assisted high-level government officials on a daily basis, including leadership in Deputy Chief's special projects in Washington, DC
- Developed, wrote, & edited materials for national publication
- Developed & maintained all databases
- Handled all office procurement including government credit cards & billing

EDUCATION

B.S. in Communications, Grand Valley State University, December 1999
Graduated magna cum laude
Paid for 100 percent of education, worked 30+ hours/week with a full class load

COMPUTER EXPERIENCE

Entire Microsoft Office Suite 2003, including Word, PowerPoint, Access, & Excel
Numerous customized databases, layout software, ACT, GELCO, & ADMARC
Knowledge of a variety of online research resources

References available upon request.

FUNCTIONAL RESUME

JEFFREY CROSS

4901 Main Street, #242
Evanston, IL 60202
(847) 555-3877
J.Cross@xxx.com

JOB OBJECTIVE

Seeking a position as a manager of a housewares department of a major department store in which I can use my talents as a manager and a salesperson.

ACHIEVEMENTS

- Promoted from customer service representative to salesperson to assistant manager in housewares at Marshall Field's.
- Managed a staff of five, performing all hiring, job training, and supervision.
- Helped to reorganize inventory control methods.
- Assisted customers in choosing housewares and conducted sales transactions.
- Combined managerial and sales talents to increase department sales figures.

WORK EXPERIENCE

Marshall Field's, Skokie, IL
Assistant Manager, 2004 - Present
Salesperson, 2002 - 2004
Customer Service Representative, 2001 - 2002

Peters Hardware, Evanston, IL
Stock Clerk, Summers, 1999 - 2001

EDUCATION

Oakton Community College, Des Plaines, IL
A.S. in Business, June 2004

References available upon request.

- Always try to fit your resume on one page. If you are having trouble with this, you may be trying to say too much. Edit out any repetitive or unnecessary information, and shorten descriptions of earlier jobs where possible. Ask a friend you trust for feedback on what seems unnecessary or unimportant. For example, you may have included too many optional sections. Today, with the prevalence of the personal computer as a tool, there is no excuse for a poorly laid out resume. Experiment with variations until you are pleased with the result.

Remember that a resume is not an autobiography. Too much information will only get in the way. The more compact your resume, the easier it will be to review. If a person who is swamped with resumes looks at yours, catches the main points, and then calls you for an interview to fill in some of the details, your resume has already accomplished its task. A clear and concise resume makes for a happy reader and a good impression.

There are times when, despite extensive editing, the resume simply cannot fit on one page. In this case, the resume should be laid out on two pages in such a way that neither clarity nor appearance is compromised. Each page of a two-page resume should be marked clearly: the first should indicate "Page 1 of 2," and the second should include your name and the page number, for example, "Julia Ramirez—Page 2 of 2." The pages should then be paper-clipped together. You may use a smaller type size (in the same font as the body of your resume) for the page numbers. Place them at the bottom of page one and the top of page two. Again, spend the time now to experiment with the layout until you find one that looks good to you.

Always show your final layout to other people and ask them what they like or dislike about it, and what impresses them most when they read your resume. Make sure that their responses are the same as what you want to elicit from your prospective employer. If they aren't the same, you should continue to make changes until the necessary information is emphasized.

Proofreading

After you have finished typing the master copy of your resume and before you have it copied or printed, thoroughly check it for typing and spelling errors. Do not place all your trust in your computer's spellcheck function. Use an old editing trick and read the whole resume backward—start at the end and read it right to left and bottom to top. This can help you see the small errors or inconsistencies that are easy to overlook. Take time to do it right because a single error on a document this important can cause the reader to judge your attention to detail in a harsh light.

Have several people look at the finished resume just in case you've missed an error. Don't try to take a shortcut; not having an unbiased set of eyes examine your resume now could mean embarrassment later. Even experienced editors can easily overlook their own errors. Be thorough and conscientious with your proofreading so your first impression is a perfect one.

We have included the following rules of capitalization and punctuation to assist you in the final stage of creating your resume. Remember that resumes often require use of a shorthand style of writing that may include sentences without periods and other stylistic choices that break the standard rules of grammar. Be consistent in each section and throughout the whole resume with your choices.

RULES OF CAPITALIZATION

- Capitalize proper nouns, such as names of schools, colleges, and universities; names of companies; and brand names of products.

- Capitalize major words in the names and titles of books, tests, and articles that appear in the body of your resume.

- Capitalize words in major section headings of your resume.

- Do not capitalize words just because they seem important.

- When in doubt, consult a style manual such as *Words into Type* (Prentice Hall) or *The Chicago Manual of Style* (The University of Chicago Press). Your local library can help you locate these and other reference books. Many computer programs also have grammar help sections.

RULES OF PUNCTUATION

- Use commas to separate words in a series.

- Use a semicolon to separate series of words that already include commas within the series. (For an example, see the first rule of capitalization.)

- Use a semicolon to separate independent clauses that are not joined by a conjunction.

- Use a period to end a sentence.

- Use a colon to show that examples or details follow that will expand or amplify the preceding phrase.

- Avoid the use of dashes.

- Avoid the use of brackets.

- If you use any punctuation in an unusual way in your resume, be consistent in its use.

- Whenever you are uncertain, consult a style manual.

Putting Your Resume in Print

You will need to buy high-quality paper for your printer before you print your finished resume. Regular office paper is not good enough for resumes; the reviewer will probably think it looks flimsy and cheap. Go to an office supply store or copy shop and select a high-quality bond paper that will make a good first impression. Select colors like white, off-white, or possibly a light gray. In some industries, a pastel may be acceptable, but be sure the color and feel of the paper make a subtle, positive statement about you. Nothing in the choice of paper should be loud or unprofessional.

If your computer printer does not reproduce your resume properly and produces smudged or stuttered type, either ask to borrow a friend's or take your disk (or a clean original) to a printer or copy shop for high-quality copying. If you anticipate needing a large number of copies, taking your resume to a copy shop or a printer is probably the best choice.

Hold a sheet of your unprinted bond paper up to the light. If it has a watermark, you will want to point this out to the person helping you with copies; the printing should be done so that the reader can read the print and see the watermark the right way up. Check each copy for smudges or streaks. This is the time to be a perfectionist—the results of your careful preparation will be well worth it.

The Cover Letter

Once your resume has been assembled, laid out, and printed to your satisfaction, the next and final step before distribution is to write your cover letter. Though there may be instances where you deliver your resume in person, you will usually send it through the mail or online. Resumes sent through the mail always need an accompanying letter that briefly introduces you and your resume. The purpose of the cover letter is to get a potential employer to read your resume, just as the purpose of the resume is to get that same potential employer to call you for an interview.

Like your resume, your cover letter should be clean, neat, and direct. A cover letter usually includes the following information:

1. Your name and address (unless it already appears on your personal letterhead) and your phone number(s); see item 7.

2. The date.

3. The name and address of the person and company to whom you are sending your resume.

4. The salutation ("Dear Mr." or "Dear Ms." followed by the person's last name, or "To Whom It May Concern" if you are answering a blind ad).

5. An opening paragraph explaining why you are writing (for example, in response to an ad, as a follow-up to a previous meeting, at the suggestion of someone you both know) and indicating that you are interested in whatever job is being offered.

6. One or more paragraphs that tell why you want to work for the company and what qualifications and experiences you can bring to the position. This is a good place to mention some detail about

that particular company that makes you want to work for them; this shows that you have done some research before applying.

7. A final paragraph that closes the letter and invites the reviewer to contact you for an interview. This can be a good place to tell the potential employer which method would be best to use when contacting you. Be sure to give the correct phone number and a good time to reach you, if that is important. You may mention here that your references are available upon request.

8. The closing ("Sincerely" or "Yours truly") followed by your signature in a dark ink, with your name typed under it.

Your cover letter should include all of this information and be no longer than one page in length. The language used should be polite, businesslike, and to the point. Don't attempt to tell your life story in the cover letter; a long and cluttered letter will serve only to annoy the reader. Remember that you need to mention only a few of your accomplishments and skills in the cover letter. The rest of your information is available in your resume. If your cover letter is a success, your resume will be read and all pertinent information reviewed by your prospective employer.

Producing the Cover Letter

Cover letters should always be individualized because they are always written to specific individuals and companies. Never use a form letter for your cover letter or copy it as you would a resume. Each cover letter should be unique, and as personal and lively as possible. (Of course, once you have written and rewritten your first cover letter until you are satisfied with it, you can certainly use similar wording in subsequent letters. You may want to save a template on your computer for future reference.) Keep a hard copy of each cover letter so you know exactly what you wrote in each one.

There are sample cover letters in Chapter 6. Use them as models or for ideas of how to assemble and lay out your own cover letters. Remember that every letter is unique and depends on the particular circumstances of the individual writing it and the job for which he or she is applying.

After you have written your cover letter, proofread it as thoroughly as you did your resume. Again, spelling or punctuation errors are a sure sign of carelessness, and you don't want that to be a part of your first impression on a prospective employer. This is no time to trust your spellcheck function. Even after going through a spelling and grammar check, your cover letter should be carefully proofread by at least one other person.

Print the cover letter on the same quality bond paper you used for your resume. Remember to sign it, using a good dark-ink pen. Handle the letter and resume carefully to avoid smudging or wrinkling, and mail them together in an appropriately sized envelope. Many stores sell matching envelopes to coordinate with your choice of bond paper.

Keep an accurate record of all resumes you send out and the results of each mailing. This record can be kept on your computer, in a calendar or notebook, or on file cards. Knowing when a resume is likely to have been received will keep you on track as you make follow-up phone calls.

About a week after mailing resumes and cover letters to potential employers, contact them by telephone. Confirm that your resume arrived and ask whether an interview might be possible. Be sure to record the name of the person you spoke to and any other information you gleaned from the conversation. It is wise to treat the person answering the phone with a great deal of respect; sometimes the assistant or receptionist has the ear of the person doing the hiring.

You should make a great impression with the strong, straightforward resume and personalized cover letter you have just created. We wish you every success in securing the career of your dreams!

Sample Resumes

This chapter contains dozens of sample resumes for people pursuing a wide variety of jobs and careers.

There are many different styles of resumes in terms of graphic layout and presentation of information. These samples represent people with varying amounts of education and experience. Use them as models for your own resume. Choose one resume or borrow elements from several different resumes to help you design your own.

DANIEL KEYS

548 West Hollywood Way • Burbank, CA 91505
(818) 555-9090 • Dan_Keys@xxx.com

OBJECTIVE

Obtain an upper-level management position in the record industry where I can employ my sales, marketing, and promotion experience.

EXPERIENCE

WARNER BROTHERS RECORDS, Burbank, CA
Director, Marketing—Jazz Department, 4/03–Present
• Develop and implement strategic marketing plans for new releases and catalog.
• Produce reissue packages and samplers for both retail and promotion.
• Write and edit ad copy.
• Interface with creative services and national print and radio.
• Oversee all aspects of sales.
• Coordinate promotional activities and chart reports.

I.R.S. RECORDS, Los Angeles, CA
National Sales Manager, 8/99–4/03
West Coast Sales Manager, 9/96–8/99
• Increased sales profile, specifically West Coast retailers, one-stops, and racks.
• Promoted to National Sales Manager, where I established sales and promotion program.
• Coordinated radio and chart reports.

SPECIALTY RECORDS, Scranton, PA
Sales Representative, 1/95–8/96
• Handled sales, merchandising, and account servicing for LPs and cassettes.
• Called on major chains and small independent retailers.
• Promoted new releases and maintained account inventory.

TOWER RECORDS, Los Angeles, CA
Manager, 8/94–1/95
• Handled sales, merchandising, customer service, product selection and ordering, and personnel management and supervision for a full-line retail outlet.

MCA RECORDS DISTRIBUTION, Universal City, CA
Sales Representative, 9/88–8/94
• Promoted and sold MCA product to Los Angeles and surrounding counties.
• Designed in-store window displays.
• Coordinated media advertising support programs.

EDUCATION

University of California, Berkeley—Berkeley, CA
B.A., Liberal Arts, June 1988

References available.

Carol Gherkin

4432 W. Simpson St.
Minneapolis, MN 44515
cgherkin@xxx.com
(612) 555-4342

Job Objective

Seeking a sales position with a pharmaceutical company that services hospitals in which I can utilize my education, communication skills, and sales experience.

Experience

Sales Representative, PHARMED, INC., St. Paul, MN, 2/03 to Present
- Demonstrate and explain new drugs to physicians.
- Handle follow-ups and updates on products.
- Increased sales by 30 percent in my first two years.
- Train and monitor new sales representatives.

Sales Trainee, HOSPO SUPPLY COMPANY, Edina, MN, 4/02 to 2/03
- Determined which drugs were necessary for stocking hospital supply rooms.
- Handled stocking for previously established orders.
- Increased staff awareness of new products.

Education

M.S., University of Minnesota, Chemistry, 2002
B.S., Iowa State University, Chemistry, 2000

Seminiars

"Presenting New Drugs to In-Office Physicians," Sales and Marketing Professionals' Association, 2002

Honors

- Raymond Johnson Chemistry Award, 2002
- Phi Beta Kappa, 2000
- Dean's List, 1999, 2000

Activities

Chemistry Club, 2002
Biology Club, 1999 to 2000

REFERENCES AVAILABLE

RAMON ZARET

827 North Willow Street
Modesto, CA 55824
Cellular: 346-555-4999
E-mail: rzaret@xxx.com

OBJECTIVE   To obtain a position as the Public Relations Director for
                       a major beverage company.

EXPERIENCE   Coca-Cola, Inc., Modesto, CA
                       National Sales Manager, 2002 to Present
                       Account Manager, 2000 to 2002
                       Assistant Account Manager, 1997 to 2000

- Manage a sales staff that includes account managers and sales representatives.
- Monitor the effectiveness of a national distribution network.
- Present new products to clients and retailers.
- Design convention displays.
- Oversee all aspects of sales and marketing budgets.
- Organize focus groups to identify new options for products.
- Develop ads, posters, and point-of-purchase materials for products.

EDUCATION   American University, White Plains, NY
                       B.A. in English, 1997

SEMINARS   American Marketing Association Seminars, 2000 to 2003
                       Coca-Cola Internal Sales Workshops, 2001 to 2003
                       Soft Drink Industry Conventions

References on request.

PEDRO GONZALES

759 Pullman Road • El Paso, TX 67751
P.Gonzales@xxx.net • (982) 555-4560

OBJECTIVE

To obtain a position as a sales representative to utilize my sales and communication skills.

WORK HISTORY

Belwin-Mills, Inc., El Paso, TX
Salesperson, 2002 to Present
- Sell sheet music to retail businesses.
- Maintain monthly expenses and yearly budgets.
- Named top salesperson of 2002.
- Maintain excellent customer relations by identifying and meeting customer needs.
- Manage extensive database and electronic files on current and potential customers.
- Incorporate new technology into sales research and sales calls.
- Train new sales representatives and advise them on effective selling techniques.

Fuller Brush Company, Austin, TX
Salesperson, 1997 to 2002
- Sold products for the home in the south Austin area.
- Increased territory sales by 65 percent in five years.
- Demonstrated and planned specific uses for household products.
- Maintained constant contact with accounts.

EDUCATION

Fuller Brush Training Course, Austin, TX
Summer 1997

Barton Technical High School, Dallas, TX
Graduated 1997

COMPUTER SKILLS

- Proficient with the entire Microsoft Office Suite, including Word, PowerPoint, Access, and Excel.
- Familiar with numerous database programs.
- Knowledge of a variety of online research resources.

References available upon request.

LATISHA BROWN

788 Robinson Drive
Lansing, MI 48061
lbrown@xxx.com
(989) 555-5401

JOB OBJECTIVE	Entry-level sales position.
EDUCATION	M.B.A. in Marketing, June 2004 Michigan State University, East Lansing, MI B.S. in Finance, 2002 University of Colorado, Boulder, CO
HONORS	Summa Cum Laude, 2004 Dean's List, 2001, 2002
WORK HISTORY	HOPPER MANUFACTURING, East Lansing, MI Administrative Assistant/Sales Department August 2004 to Present • Assist account executives with general correspon-dence, data entry, and sales proposals. • Set up and staff displays at industry trade shows. • Maintain budgets for the sales staff. • Develop and maintain databases. Sales Trainee, Summer 2003 • Assisted with billing, orders, and inventory. • Shipped orders and assured delivery. • Made travel and entertainment arrangements for sales staff.
REFERENCES	Available on request.

SHAWANA HODGES

5678 North Riverside Drive ✦ Hartford, WA 91505
(818) 555-8989 ✦ shawanahodges@xxx.com

CAREER OBJECTIVE
Sales representative for an office supplies company.

ACHIEVEMENTS
✦ Handled price quotations, information on product line, and special orders.
✦ Assisted sales manager in establishing and streamlining standard office procedures.
✦ Arranged travel, accommodations, and scheduling of seminars and meetings.
✦ Drafted monthly reports on sales procedures and profit margins.
✦ Managed office records.
✦ Delegated editing duties and proofreading responsibilities.
✦ Supervised two student interns.

WORK HISTORY
Sanco Office Supplies, Ltd., Hartford, WA
Executive Secretary to Sales Manager, 2002–Present

Popular Artists, Management, Pasadena, CA
Secretary to Manager of Publications, 1998–2002

EDUCATION
Pasadena College, Pasadena, CA
B.S. in Marketing, 2002
Evening Division

Commercial School of Business, Los Angeles, CA
Completed advanced secretarial course.

SKILLS
✦ Full knowledge of Microsoft Office.
✦ Typing speed: 55 wpm.
✦ Strong grasp of online research resources.

References available on request.

Jennifer Sungentuk

1314 Beaver Lake Road
Saint Paul, MN 55101
Jenny.Sungentuk@xxx.com
(332) 555-3909

Job Objective

Computer Sales

Experience

Microtech Computers, Saint Paul, MN
Account Executive, 4/99 to Present
- Handle sales accounts for northern suburban area.
- Expanded customer base by 25 percent during my tenure.
- Conduct field visits to resolve customer problems.
- Write product information fliers and distribute them through direct-mail program.

IBM, Cottage Grove, MN
Technical Support Specialist, 9/91 to 4/99
- Installed and maintained operating system.
- Performance-tuned subsystems and networks.
- Coordinated problem resolution with phone companies.
- Planned and installed new hardware and programming techniques.

IBM, Cottage Grove, MN
Systems Analyst, 2/90 to 9/91
- Documented procedures for mechanization of payroll department.
- Coordinated requirements meeting with production department on new inventory system.
- Developed test procedures for reverification of new application.
- Developed standards for electronic mail system.

Education

Winona State University, Winona, MN

M.S. in Mathematics, 1990
Graduated with honors

B.S. in Chemistry, 1988
Dean's List
Seabrook Scholarship

Affiliations

Computer Sales Association
Minnesota Business Chapter

Seminars

Microtech Sales Seminars
IBM Technical Workshop

References available on request.

HANNAH GOLDSTEIN

1800 Riverside Street
Farmington Hills, MI 48076
(586) 555-8938
H.Goldstein@xxx.com

Job Objective

A marketing/promotion position in the entertainment industry where I can utilize my communication skills, contacts, and industry knowledge.

Work Experience

TBC MARKETING, Detroit, MI
Independent Marketing, 1/03 to Present
- Coordinate stock with regional distributors.
- Generate exposure and interest at local retail stores and one-stops in conjunction with local and regional airplay.
- Suggest supplemental marketing strategies based on airplay, sales, and percentage penetration.

HITS MAGAZINE, Plymouth, MI
National Marketing Coordinator, 4/01 to 1/03
- Sold charts and tracking information to radio, artist management, and record labels.
- Handled tracking for all accounts on charting product.
- Interacted with radio accounts weekly regarding early chart information.

CASHBOX MAGAZINE, Ann Arbor, MI
Regional Sales Representative, 4/98 to 4/01
- Managed and developed West Coast territory for Cashbox Service Network.
- Provided chart information, including bullet criteria, points, and sales/airplay ratios to independent marketing companies and management.
- Serviced retail accounts and created new marketing strategies for product tracking services.

PARKER MANUFACTURING, Flint, MI
Sales Representative, 7/94 to 4/98
- Negotiated and sold contract repairs on industrial equipment.
- Wrote daily technical reports on product movement and inventory.
- Consistently met and exceeded quarterly sales quotas.

Education

Grand Valley State University, Allendale, MI
B.A., Communications, June 1994

References available on request.

Camille Diaz

300 Big Malle Road
San Antonio, TX 84038
Cell: (214) 555-8888
E-mail: Cam_Diaz@xxx.com

Objective

A management position in the sales and marketing field.

Achievements

SALES

- Increased watch sales from $3 million to $12 million during the past six years.
- Introduced new product lines through presentation to major retailers.
- Developed 15 new accounts.
- Supervised three sales agencies throughout the United States and Canada.

MARKETING

- Researched the watch market in order to coordinate product line with current fashion trends.
- Increased company's share of the market through improved quality products.

Work History

Culture Shock Watch Company, Dallas, TX
Vice President of Sales and Marketing, 1994 to Present

Nabisco Food Company, San Francisco, CA
Sales and Product Food Manager, 1989 to 1994

Avis, Inc., Los Angeles, CA
Sales Representative, 1984 to 1989

Education

University of Southern California, Los Angeles, CA
B.S. in Business Administration, 1983

Seminars

Dallas Sales and Marketing Conference, 2002, 2003
National Marketing Association Convention, 1997 to 2001

References available on request.

OMAR HUSAK

3201 W. Lovell St., Apt. 23 • Pittsburgh, PA 38901
Home: (412) 555-9302 • Cell: (412) 555-4209

JOB SOUGHT

Public relations director for the marketing division of a major candy manufacturer.

EXPERIENCE

Public Relations
■ Represented company to clients and retailers while presenting new products.
■ Assisted in design of company website.
■ Organized and planned convention displays and strategy.
■ Designed and executed direct-mail campaign that identified marketplace needs.
■ Developed new angles for representing products.

Management
■ Managed a sales/marketing staff that included account managers and sales representatives.
■ Monitored and studied the effectiveness of a national distribution network.
■ Oversaw sales/marketing budget.

Development
■ Created product advertisements.
■ Initiated and published a monthly newsletter that was distributed to current and potential customers.

WORK HISTORY

Redboy Peanut Crunch, Pittsburgh, PA
National Sales Manager, 2002-present
Account Manager, 2000-2002
Assistant Account Manager, 1999-2000
Personnel Assistant, 1997-1999
Receptionist, 1995-1997

Page 1 of 2

EDUCATION

B.A. in English, 1995
University of Pennsylvania, Harrisburg, PA

SEMINARS

American Marketing Association Seminars, 2000-2003

COMPUTER SKILLS

- Various wireless technologies, including Palm and Blackberry.
- Database development and management.
- Layout and design software, including PageMaker, Photoshop, and Publisher.
- Strong background with the Internet as a sales and research tool.

REFERENCES

Available on request.

Jennifer Nguyen

35 Desert Rose Way   Las Vegas, NV 46331   JenniferNguyen@xxx.com
(714) 555-6789

Objective
Full-time sales position that will allow me to use my sales, customer service, and design skills to benefit an established jewelry store.

Overview
Several years of experience selling custom-made jewelry.
Excellent customer service record.
Ability to resolve customer complaints to the satisfaction of customers and employers.
Generate repeat business by establishing rapport with customers.
Design creative, effective jewelry displays.
Strong attention to detail in entering computer data and managing inventory.

Work Experience
Stacey's Jewelers, Las Vegas, NV
Sales Associate, January 2003–Present

Eddy Gems, Las Vegas, NV
Salesclerk, April 2000–December 2002

Jones Day Care, Tempe, AZ
Art Teacher, February 1998–April 2000

Parker Hardware, Robeson, AZ
Cashier, May 1996–February 1998

Education
Tempe College, Tempe, AZ
B.A. in Art, January 1998

Honors
Tempe Honor Society, 1998
Velma G. Lydeckker Art Award, 1997

Special Skills
Fluent in Spanish.
Computer experience, including jewelry design programs.
Knowledge of semiprecious stones and metals.

References
Available on request.

DEREK WASHINGTON

453 Franklin Ave.
Saint Louis, MO 63140
dwashington@xxx.net
(619) 555-3489

Career Objective

A management position in marketing utilizing my promotion and public relations experience.

Work Experience

JUST PASTA, INC., Saint Louis, MO
Marketing Director, 2001 to Present
- Supervise a successful marketing campaign for a restaurant chain.
- Initiate and maintain a positive working relationship with print media.
- Implement numerous marketing strategies to increase sales at less-profitable outlets.
- Developed and administered a training program for store managers and staff.

GREAT IDEAS CARPET CLEANING COMPANY, Jefferson City, MO
Marketing Representative, 1997 to 2001
- Demonstrated carpet cleaners in specialty and department stores.
- Designed fliers and advertising to promote products.
- Performed frequent calls to retail outlets.

REBO CHIPS, Jefferson City, MO
Assistant Sales Manager, 1992 to 1997
- Handled both internal and external areas of sales and marketing, including samples, advertising, and pricing.
- Served as company sales representative and sold products to retail outlets.

Education

Baker University, Lee's Summit, MO
B.A. in Marketing, 1992

Seminars

Washington University Marketing Workshop, 2003
Sales and Marketing Association Seminars, 1999

References Available

Mary Alice Moore

3230 Alsip Court, #3C

Milwaukee, WI 53100

M.A.Moore@xxx.com

(419) 555-8908

Objective

Marketing representative for a major U.S. airline.

Experience

Midwest Airlines, Inc., Milwaukee, WI
Sales Representative, 2/03 - Present
- Sell reservations for domestic flights, hotels, and car rentals.
- Market travel packages through travel agencies.
- Negotiate airline and hotel discounts for customers.
- Devise itineraries and solve customers' travel-related problems.

Travel the World, Kenosha, WI
Travel Agent, 6/95 - 2/03
- Handled customer reservations for airlines, hotels, and car rentals.
- Advised customers on competitive travel packages and prices.
- Interacted with all major airlines, hotel chains, and car rental companies.

Education

University of Wisconsin, Beloit, WI
B.A. in Anthropology, 1995

Skills

- Extensive experience using most travel-related computer systems, including Apollo.
- Working knowledge of German, French, and Polish.
- Strong computer and multiline phone system background.

References on request.

■ MICHELLE WONG ■

1156 Oceanview Road
Saint Petersburg, FL 22451
m-wong@xxx.com
(324) 555-4727

■ OBJECTIVE
Entry-level sales position

■ EDUCATION
University of Florida, Gainesville, FL
Bachelor of Science in Economics
Expected June 2005
GPA: 3.45

■ HONORS
Phi Beta Kappa
Dean's List, seven quarters
Owen L. Coon Award, Honorable Mention

■ ACTIVITIES
President, Activities and Organizations Board
Wa-Mu Show
Captain, Soccer Team
Freshman Advisor

■ WORK EXPERIENCE
Shand Morihand Insurance Company, Fort Lauderdale, FL
Marketing Intern, 2004
Assisted marketing staff in the areas of research and sales forecasts designed
to identify new customers and direct promotion.

University of Florida, Gainesville, FL
Student Assistant, Registrar's Office, 2003–2004
Processed transcript requests.
Entered registrations into the computer.
Provided students with basic information regarding registration.

■ SKILLS
Knowledge of French and Russian
Experience with Microsoft Office Suite
Familiar with both Mac and PC formats

References available upon request

JEREMY HOEFNER

1441 Gilbert Street • Providence, RI 00231
Jeremy.Hoefner@xxx.com • (401) 555-3782

OBJECTIVE

To capitalize on my extensive management, promotion, and sales experience in
an executive-level position in the publishing industry.

EMPLOYMENT HISTORY

JOHNSON PUBLISHING CORPORATION, Providence, RI
Vice President, 1997–2005
Promoted from sales manager to vice president of advertising after three
years. Managed all phases of publishing properties, including:
Furniture Magazine
Home Improvement Weekly
Scuba Digest
Travel Age Magazine
Pharmacy News
Established and developed the first newspaper advertising mat service in the
furniture industry. Increased distributors and retailers using this service by
55 percent in three years. Improved the effectiveness and volume of all retail
advertising.

REBUS PUBLISHING COMPANY, Boston, MA
Advertising Manager, 1988–1997
Serviced and developed accounts throughout the eastern United States.
Handled advertising for publications in the restaurant industry. Increased
sales in my territories every year by at least 21 percent.

TIME MAGAZINE, New York, NY
Assistant Advertising Promotion Manager, 1984–1988
Spearheaded original promotion program that increased revenue 33 percent in
two years. Developed and grew new markets. Helped to improve customer and
company relations.

ROYAL CROWN COLA CORPORATION, Chicago, IL
Division Sales Manager, 1981–1984
Promoted from salesperson to sales manager after one year. Organized sampling campaigns and in-store and restaurant displays. Directed bottlers' cooperative advertising and point-of-purchase displays.

EDUCATION
DRAKE UNIVERSITY, Des Moines, IA
B.A., Communications, 1981
Graduated Phi Beta Kappa
Top 5 percent of class

PROFESSIONAL AFFILIATIONS
Rocking Chair, President, 2002–Present
Publishers Association, Advisory Committee, 1997–Present
Beverage Association of America, Board of Directors, 1982–1984

REFERENCES
Available upon request.

DIANA FAGEN THOMPSON
8000 E. Fifth Ave.
Silver Spring, MD 20905
dthompson2@xxx.com
410-555-4988

<u>**OBJECTIVE**</u>	A management position in sales or marketing.
<u>**WORK HISTORY**</u>	**INTERCO, WASHINGTON, DC** Regional Sales Manager, 2001–Present • Manage sales in eastern markets for a manufacturer of cotton products. • Represent four corporate divisions of the company, with sales in excess of $2 million annually. • Direct and motivate a sales force of 12 to achieve company goals. **ROBERTSON COMPANY, MIAMI, FL** District Manager, 1996–2001 • Acted as sales representative for the Miami metropolitan area. • Built both wholesale and dealer distribution substantially during my tenure. • Developed monthly sales plans that identified necessary account maintenance and specific problems that required attention. **WESTERN SPORTS PRODUCTS, SARASOTA, FL** Assistant Sales Manager, 1993–1996 • Handled both internal and external areas of sales and marketing, including samples, advertising, and pricing. • Sold a variety of sports equipment to retail stores.
<u>**EDUCATION**</u>	University of Miami, Miami, FL B.A. in English, 1993
<u>**SEMINARS**</u>	American Sales Association Seminars, 1993–2004
<u>**REFERENCES**</u>	Available on request.

TYRELL JACOBS

4504 Bloomfield Avenue
White Plains, NY 12090
tyrelljacobs@xxx.com
(914) 555-3849

JOB OBJECTIVE
A management-level sales position within the plastics industry.

PROFESSIONAL EXPERIENCE
Clear Plastics, Inc., Brooklyn, NY
Sales Manager, 2000–present
Sell custom-designed point-of-purchase elements and product displays. Research target areas and develop new account leads. Research and determine advertising in national publications. Make sales presentations to potential customers. Participate in plastics industry trade shows.

Westchester Tractor Company, Westchester, NY
District Sales Manager, 1996–2000
Planned successful sales strategies to identify and develop new accounts. Supervised seven sales representatives. Researched and analyzed market conditions to seek out new customers. Wrote monthly sales reports.

Brooklyn Freight Company, Brooklyn, NY
Account Executive, 1993–1996
Managed accounts in the New York metropolitan area. Expanded customer service base 30 percent in four years. Monitored customer satisfaction with product and service. Developed training program for new hires.

EDUCATION
Harvard University, Boston, MA
M.B.A. with honors, 1992

Drake University, Des Moines, IA
B.A. in Accounting, 1989

PROFESSIONAL MEMBERSHIPS
Brooklyn Sales Association, 2003–present
New York Merchants Group, 1996–present

REFERENCES
Available on request.

Maria Sabatini

45 E. 45th St., Apt. 414
Minneapolis, MN 50290
m.sabatini@xxx.net
(612) 555-3490

JOB OBJECTIVE

A position as a sales/marketing representative for a manufacturer of musical instruments.

PROFESSIONAL ACHIEVEMENTS

Sales

- Established and maintained an excellent relationship with more than 100 accounts in the musical instrument industry.
- Acted as a liaison between customers and company.
- Provided customers with detailed information on products and replacement parts.
- Named salesperson of the month six times.

Marketing

- Demonstrated to customers the value of quality purchases.
- Researched industry competition to refine and strengthen marketing techniques.
- Projected success of new products through surveys and questionnaires.
- Studied demographics and customized deck for presentations to potential clients.

WORK HISTORY

Roland Corporation, Minneapolis, MN
Sales Representative, 2002–present

Twin Cities Electronics, St. Paul, MN
Salesperson, 1999–2002

EDUCATION

Milton Community College, Edina, MN
A.S. degree in Business, May 1999

REFERENCES AVAILABLE

Terrence Johnson

5656 Prairie Road
Chicago, IL 60189
terry.johnson@xxx.com
(773) 555-1828

Objective: Full-time, management-level sales and marketing position.

Professional Achievements

- Introduced new and existing product lines to major clients.
- Increased sales from $27 million to $50 million in five years.
- Initiated and developed seven new accounts.
- Supervised three sales agencies throughout the United States.
- Researched computer market in order to coordinate product line with current buying trends.
- Developed new approaches to marketing software products.

Employment History

Ranco Computer Company, Chicago, IL
Sales and Marketing Manager, 2001–present

Unico, Melrose Park, IL
Product Coordinator, 1991–2001

Torvis Electrical Supply, Canoga Falls, NY
Sales Representative, 1986–1991

Education

University of Oklahoma, Norman, OK
B.S., Business Administration, June 1986
Minor: Computer Science

References: Available on request.

AIMEE DYKSTRA

66 Mountain Crest Trail
Salt Lake City, UT 90056
(385) 555-7200

OBJECTIVE
Sales Manager Position

WORK EXPERIENCE
Pier One Imports, Salt Lake City, UT
Sales Coordinator, 2003 to Present
- Manage 10 field representatives.
- Disseminate information on company policies, sales goals, and strategies.
- Place advertising in major trade publications.
- Promote products at trade shows.
- Maintain inventory status reports and personnel records.

Auburn Publishing Company, West Jordan, UT
Distribution Assistant, 1996 to 2003
- Developed new distribution outlets through cold calls and follow-up visits.
- Increased distribution in Utah district by 45 percent over a three-year period.
- Coordinated a direct-mail program that increased magazine subscriptions 120 percent.

Canon Company, Atlanta, GA
Sales Representative, 1991 to 1996
- Sold and serviced office copiers to businesses and schools in the greater Atlanta area.
- Maintained good customer relations through frequent calls and visits.
- Identified potential customers.

EDUCATION
Clark Atlanta University, Atlanta, GA
B.A. in English, June 1991

PROFESSIONAL MEMBERSHIPS
- National Association of Importers
- Salt Lake City Community Association
- Lion's Club

References available on request.

grisette allman

1202 Sapphire Avenue
Olympia, WA 54771
grisetteallman@xxx.com
(433) 555-8909

overview

Experienced salesperson with managerial background. Seeking a position in sales management with a major retailer that will allow me to use and expand my sales and marketing skills.

work history

Grandy's Shoes, Seattle, WA
Assistant Manager, 4/03-Present
Serve as assistant manager of a quality shoe store with partial supervision of a staff of six. Track customers' buying habits and analyze market trends. Handle promotion and mailings for special sales and in-store events. Open and close store on weekends and manage cash and bank deposits. Handle all computer tasks including database, Word, and Excel documents.

Flaherty Jewelers, Seattle, WA
Salesperson, 1/96-4/03
Sold jewelry at a fine jewelry store. Answered customer questions regarding all aspects of the product. Tracked inventory on computer. Stocked inventory within the store. Kept store clean and orderly. Trained new hires on sales techniques and use of cash register. Handled returns and orders from distributors. Designed displays for store.

Canon Company, Olympia, WA
Salesperson, 8/91-1/96
Sold copiers to schools and businesses in the greater Seattle area. Explained product features and terms of sale at on-site sales presentations. Expanded customer base through intensive cold calling in person and over the phone.

education

Olympia Community College, Olympia, WA
Attended two years, majoring in Business.

Central High School, Olympia, WA
Graduated 1991.

References available.

STEVEN JUNG
76 N. Washington Blvd. • Houston, TX 72009
steve.jung@xxx.com
(714) 555-4890

GOAL
A position as a sales representative that involves direct sales and account management.

WORK EXPERIENCE
Salesperson, 2003–Present, R&G Sugar, Inc., Houston, TX
• Sell refined sugar products to retail businesses.
• Maintain good customer relations by identifying customer needs.
• Train new sales representatives and advise them on effective selling techniques.
• Named top salesperson of 2002.

Salesperson, 1998–2003, Popson Camera Company, Milwaukee, WI
• Sold cameras to retail outfits in the south suburban Milwaukee area.
• Increased territory sales by 85 percent in five years.
• Planned and demonstrated specific uses for products in various offices.
• Maintained contact with accounts.

EDUCATION
Popson Sales Training Course, Milwaukee, WI
Summer 1998

Cobert Technical High School, West Allis, WI
Graduated 1997
Football Team Co-captain

REFERENCES
Available on request.

JANE ESPOSITO

1814 N. Seminola Ave.
Cleveland, OH 47889
J.Esposito@xxx.com
(216) 555-3400

CAREER OBJECTIVE

To become a sales representative for an office supplies manufacturer.

EMPLOYMENT HISTORY

Tempo Office Supply Company, Cleveland, OH
Executive Secretary to Sales Manager, 2002 - Present
- Assist sales manager in various office activities and procedures.
- Handle price quotations, customer inquiries on shipments, and special orders.
- Arrange travel and transportation and schedule seminars and meetings.
- Manage computerization of the office records.

James Plastics, St. Louis, MO
Secretary to Manager of Publications, 2000 - 2002
- Arranged conferences for the department.
- Dealt directly with staff members on a variety of matters, including routing editing duties and proofreading responsibilities.
- Edited and proofread interoffice memos and a weekly department newsletter.
- Arranged for printing and distribution.

EDUCATION

Cleveland University, Cleveland, OH
B.S. in Marketing, 2004

St. Louis School of Business, St. Louis, MO
A.S. in Office Technology, 1999

SPECIAL SKILLS

- Proficiency in Microsoft Word, PowerPoint, and Excel.
- Fluent in Spanish.
- Familiar with both Mac and PC formats.
- Knowledge of Internet and ability to update websites.

REFERENCES

Furnished upon request.

Lynda Weinstein

3302 Harbor Drive, #45   Ft. Lauderdale, FL 33020
L.Weinstein@xxx.net   (305) 555-8903

Career Objective

A management position in sales and marketing.

Work Experience

South Florida Boat Company, Miami, FL
District Sales Manager, 2001 - present
❱ Plan successful strategies to identify and develop new accounts.
❱ Research and analyze market conditions in order to seek out new customers.
❱ Increased sales by at least 20 percent each year (45 percent in 2003).
❱ Develop weekly and monthly sales strategies.

Miami Industrial Supply, Miami, FL
Account Executive, 1999 - 2001
❱ Responsible for south Florida territory.
❱ Developed 23 new accounts during a two-year period.
❱ Resolved customer complaints.
❱ Provided feedback to production and shipping departments that improved customer service.
❱ Rewrote product catalog.
❱ Updated customer database.
❱ Implemented new system for standard reorders.
❱ Trained department clerical assistants.

Harrison Pany, Inc., Denver, CO
Sales Representative, 1998 - 1999
❱ Sold and serviced office copiers to Denver area businesses and schools.
❱ Designed and disbursed customer satisfaction surveys.
❱ Attended trade shows to analyze and select new product.
❱ Expanded customer base through successful direct-mail marketing campaign.

Education

University of Colorado, Boulder, CO
B.A., June 1998
Major: Economics

Professional Memberships

South Florida Sales Associates, Treasurer, 2003 - present.
Miami Chamber of Commerce, 2001 - present.

References available on request.

MARGARET MALONEY

331 Maple Avenue
Seattle, WA 99449
m-maloney@xxx.com
206/555-3898 (Home)
206/555-4444 (Cellular)

OBJECTIVE

Obtain a management position at a clothing retailer.

WORK EXPERIENCE

AVON DRESS SHOP, Seattle, WA
Assistant Manager, 2002 to Present
- Manage and update store website online.
- Sell dresses, attend to customers, advise on style, handle special orders, and take care of returned merchandise.
- Assist in design and set-up of window displays.
- Oversee the placement of ads for major advertising campaigns.
- Represent store at conventions and street fairs.
- Maintain store training and sales manual.
- Provide all aspects of training to new hires.
- Handle purchasing of garments from suppliers.

QUALITY BOUTIQUE, Tall Oaks, WA
Salesperson, 2001 to 2002
- Sold accessories to customers, handled special orders, and organized and arranged inventory.
- Handled customer returns and special requests.
- Coordinated appointments for dress fittings with seamstress and customer.
- Designed window displays.

EDUCATION

TALL OAKS HIGH SCHOOL, Tall Oaks, WA
Graduated, June 2001
- Ranked 14 in class of 300.
- Member of tennis team.
- Numerous computer classes completed.

REFERENCES

Provided on request.

Gina Kershaw

5001 Lincoln Drive • Marlton, NJ 08053
gina.kershaw@xxx.com • (609) 555-3893

OBJECTIVE

Sales manager of a paper products company.

PROFESSIONAL EXPERIENCE

HARRISON PAPER COMPANY, Philadelphia, PA
District Sales Manager, 2001–Present
- Plan successful strategies to identify and develop new accounts.
- Have increased sales by at least 20 percent each year.
- Research and analyze market conditions to find new customers.
- Supervise seven sales representatives.

DANIEL P. MILLER & COMPANY, Trenton, NJ
Sales Representative, 1994–2001
- Developed and managed new territories.
- Built sales through calls on retailers and wholesalers.
- Developed creative techniques for increasing product sales.
- Maintained current knowledge of competitive products.
- Wrote weekly and monthly sales reports.

SAMMY'S BEST BURGER COMPANY, Newark, NJ
Assistant to Sales Manager, 1987–1994
- Handled sales and marketing.
- Served as company sales representative and sold a variety of products to retail stores.
- Filled last-minute orders and delivered them personally.

EDUCATION

NEW JERSEY STATE UNIVERSITY, Trenton, NJ
- B.S. in Business, 1986
- Graduated in top 10 percent of class.
- Recipient of Floyd T. Harper Scholarship.

SPECIAL SKILLS

- Knowledge of Russian.
- Strong computer skills.
- Public speaking background.

References available on request.

HARRIET SCHUMACHER

1414 Mountain Drive • Bozeman, MT 59715
H.Schumacher@xxx.com • (415) 555-4930

OBJECTIVE

An entry-level sales position.

EDUCATION

Montana State University
Bachelor of Science in Communications
Expected June 2005

HONORS

Beta Alpha Psi Society
Dean's List
Manley Writing Award, 2003

ACTIVITIES

Treasurer, Gamma Gamma Gamma Sorority
Homecoming Planning Committee
Alumni Welcoming Committee

WORK EXPERIENCE

AT&T, New York, NY
Marketing Intern, Summer 2004
• Assisted marketing staff in the areas of research, demographics, identifying new customers, and developing special promotions.

Montana State University
Office Assistant, Journalism School, 2002-2004
• Assisted with student registration, filing, and data entry. Arranged application materials. Assembled course packs.

SKILLS

• Strong computer background including design and website management software.
• Extensive experience with presenting proposals.
• Familiar with the *The Associated Press Stylebook*.
• Knowledge of digital photography.

References available upon request.

IVAN LINDENBURG

24 E. Saginaw Rd.   ivanlindenburg@xxx.com
Crystal Lake, IL 60203   (847) 555-3894

JOB OBJECTIVE

A position as a marketing manager where I can utilize my knowledge and experience in sales and marketing.

RELEVANT ACCOMPLISHMENTS

- Managed sales of all product lines in midwestern markets for a leading maker of textiles.
- Represented five corporate divisions of the company with sales in excess of $4 million annually.
- Directed and motivated a sales force of twelve sales representatives in planned selling toward specific goals.
- Coordinated both internal and external areas of sales and marketing for an office supply manufacturer.
- Oversaw all aspects of samples, advertising, and marketing.
- Maintained good customer relations with retail stores.

EMPLOYMENT HISTORY

Robeau Industries, Chicago, IL
Regional Sales Manager, 2/00 to present

Carolina Company, Elgin, IL
District Sales Manager, 5/95 to 2/00

Super Office Company, St. Louis, MO
Assistant to the Sales Manager, 8/90 to 5/95

Page 1 of 2

EDUCATION

University of Michigan, Ann Arbor, MI
B.A. in Business Administration, 1990
Graduated Magna Cum Laude
Major: Marketing
Minor: Spanish

SEMINARS

National Management Association Seminar, 1999
University of Chicago Seminars, 2002, 2003

PROFESSIONAL MEMBERSHIPS

Sales and Marketing Association of Chicago
National Association of Market Developers

REFERENCES

Available on request

Carmen Delgadillo

17001 E. Riverside Dr.
Burbank, CA 91505
(818) 555-3728 (Day)
(818) 555-9073 (Evening)

OBJECTIVE

Marketing management position

ACHIEVEMENTS

Marketing

- Implemented various programs, including product visuals, giveaways, and delivery of presentations.
- Conceived and developed creative product promotions.
- Designed unique advertising with innovative placements, including billboards, trade publications, and newspapers.
- Administered advertising budget.
- Represented company to both industry and media.

Sales

- Exceeded revenue goals by 41 percent last year.
- Set annual sales record in 1997 with revenues of $55 million.
- Administered a $125 million advertising budget.

Management

- Restructured Paradise Vacations, achieving #1 position in sales for the western United States.
- Wrote new policy manuals and job descriptions for all departments.
- Trained staff and managers in order to increase productivity.
- Directed the sales force in achieving and exceeding sales goals.

EMPLOYMENT HISTORY

Paradise Vacations, Burbank, CA
Senior Vice President, 2001-Present

Western Airlines, San Diego, CA
Vice President of Sales, 1998-2000
Director, Sales Department, 1995-1998

EMPLOYMENT HISTORY (CONT'D)

SAS Airlines, Los Angeles, CA
Regional Sales Manager, 1990-1995
District Sales Manager, 1986-1990
Sales Representative, 1983-1986

EDUCATION

University of Colorado, Denver, CO
M.B.A., June 1983

Rivers College, Beaver Falls, KY
B.S. in Communications, June 1981

SEMINARS

Sponsored by Pacific Marketing Institute
- International Sales and Marketing
- Domestic Sales and Marketing
- Management and Administration
- Travel Sales Incentives
- Telemarketing

REFERENCES

Available on request

Patrick H. McCoy

1701 N. Hampshire Rd.   **(317) 555-3909**
Fort Wayne, IN 46802   **PatMcCoy@xxx.com**

OBJECTIVE: A position as sales manager for a midsize manufacturer.

EXPERIENCE: NEWMARK INDUSTRIES, Fort Wayne, IN
                    Account Executive, 2002 to present

                    Manage sales accounts in northeastern Indiana territory
                    for a consumer electronics company. Expanded customer
                    base by 28 percent during the last two years. Collaborate
                    with marketing department to develop direct-mail cam-
                    paigns. Maintain accounts through daily phone contact
                    and frequent on-site visits. Train new employees.

                    POTISCO, Terre Haute, IN
                    Sales Representative, 2000 to 2002

                    Handled sales to customers, particularly contractors.
                    Priced bid estimates as required. Oversaw customer and
                    public relations that helped to build the company's image.
                    Set up office procedures where necessary.

                    HONOCO, INC., Chicago, IL
                    Sales Representative, 1995 to 2000

                    Developed and managed new territories. Built sales
                    through cold calls on physicians, hospitals, retailers, and
                    wholesalers. Researched competitive product lines. Devel-
                    oped effective promotions and sales incentives.

EDUCATION: WHEATON COLLEGE, Wheaton, IL
                    B.A. in Business, 1995

SEMINARS: Marketing Techniques Using Demographics
                    Sales and Marketing for the New Millennium
                    Marketing Strategies for Manufacturers
                    Using the Internet to Promote Products

REFERENCES: Available on request.

Michelle Hwang
5001 Providence Street
Washington, DC 02930
M.Hwang@xxx.com
(202) 555-3894

Objective: A position as marketing manager for Graphics, Inc.

Experience: BURGER WORLD, INC., Washington, DC
Marketing Director, 2003–Present
Develop successful marketing campaigns for fast-food chain. Initiated and currently maintain positive working relationship with radio, television, and print media. Implement marketing strategies to increase sales at less-profitable outlets. Manage a training program for sales managers and staff.

HI FIDELITY STEREO COMPANY, Newark, NJ
Marketing Representative, 1998–2003
Demonstrated electronic equipment in stereo and department stores. Analyzed and reported customer reactions to manufacturers. Created advertising to promote products. Call retail outlets frequently.

INTERCO, New York, NY
Sales Representative, 1991–1998
Identified clients' needs and problems and provided personalized solutions. Resolved service and billing problems. Delivered sales presentations. Identified potential customers and established new accounts.

Education: GEORGETOWN UNIVERSITY, Washington, DC
B.S. in Marketing, 1991

STERN SCHOOL OF BUSINESS, NEW YORK UNIVERSITY, New York, NY
Various marketing seminars, 1992–1994

Skills: Fluent in Korean.
Knowledge of Word, Excel, PowerPoint, and Photoshop.
Familiar with numerous e-mail programs.

References: Available.

WILLIAM CHARGOT

501 Nottingham Hill
Baton Rouge, LA 76100
billchargot@xxx.com
(310) 555-3789

JOB OBJECTIVE

A management-level position in computer sales where I can utilize my sales and
technical experience in the computer industry.

EXPERIENCE

TECHNICAL
- Installed and maintained operating systems.
- Defined and oversaw network lists and tables.
- Coordinated problem solving with phone companies.
- Installed new hardware and software.

SYSTEMS ANALYSIS
- Created standards and procedures for main accounting system.
- Coordinated requirements for new delivery system with production department.
- Developed test procedures for verification of new application.
- Developed distribution lists and user IDs for electronic mail system.

SALES
- Handled sales accounts for the Baton Rouge area.
- Conducted field visits to solve customers' problems.
- Maintained contact with customers to ensure good customer relations.
- Developed product information guides and sales manuals.

EMPLOYMENT HISTORY

MicroWorld Computers, Metairie, LA - Account Executive, 1999-Present
Apple Computers, Berkeley, CA - Technical Support Specialist, 1992-1999
Datalog Inc., St. Louis, MO - Systems Analyst, 1981-1991

EDUCATION

Xavier University, New Orleans, LA
M.S. in Mathematics, 1980

Southeastern Louisiana University, Hammond, LA
B.S. in Communications, June 1977

PROFESSIONAL AFFILIATIONS

Computer Sales Association
Louisiana Business Council
Citizens for a Cleaner Environment

SEMINARS

Apple Technical Workshops
MicroWorld Sales Seminars

REFERENCES AVAILABLE ON REQUEST

Matthew R. Clarkson

1251 Babcock Avenue
Des Moines, IA 52909
(515) 555-4999 (Day)
(515) 555-3429 (Evening)

Objective

Manager of the hardware department of a major department store.

Achievements

- Promoted from customer service representative to salesperson and then to assistant manager in hardware at Sears in Des Moines.
- Manage a staff of six, including hiring, job training, and supervision.
- Reorganize and improve inventory control methods.
- Assist customers in choosing and using hardware products.
- Combine managerial and sales talents to increase department sales.

Work History

SEARS, Des Moines, IA
Assistant Manager, March 2003 to Present
Salesperson, February 2001 to March 2003
Customer Service Representative, August 2000 to February 2001

SAM'S HARDWARE, West Petersville, IA
Stock Clerk, Summers 1998 to 2000

Education

Des Moines Township High School, Des Moines, IA
Graduated June 1990
Top 25 percent of class
Student Council Secretary
Homecoming Committee

Redbrook College, Des Moines, IA
Various night courses, including Retail Sales Management, Computer Science, and Supervisory Techniques.

References

By request.

Terrell Johnson

3240 Spring Road
Clarksville, AR 72204
T.Johnson@xxx.com
(213) 555-9832

Objective

A position as an assistant sales manager for an automobile dealer.

Skills/Accomplishments

SALES
- Identified clients' needs and problems and provided solutions
- Explained billing policies and resolved problems with outstanding accounts
- Created and delivered sales presentations
- Conducted market research and established new accounts
- Increased client base by 40 percent

DEVELOPMENT
- Researched competitive product lines and drafted reports to District Manager
- Prepared sales forecasts and sales goals reports
- Developed monthly sales plans for maintaining accounts and resolving potential problems

Employment History

Yugo America, Inc., Eureka Springs, AR
Sales Representative, 4/02 to Present

Track Autoparts, Inc., Clarksville, AR
Sales Representative, 9/00 to 4/02

Apple One Temporary, Little Rock, AR
Sales Representative, 5/99 to 9/00

Education

University of Arkansas, Little Rock, AR
B.A. in Art, 1999

References

Available on request.

GLORIA GARLAND

1220 Market Street, #3
San Francisco, CA 92290
415-555-5508
G.Garland@xxx.com

OBJECTIVE
A management-level position in the publishing industry.

WORK EXPERIENCE
BAY MAGAZINE, San Fransicso, CA
Regional Manager, 2002–present
• Oversee administration, negotiation, and maintenance of exchange agreements and sales promotion.
• Track market changes, with responsibility for executing responses to developments.
• Recently led magazine's eastern edition through a reorganization period.
• Planned and implemented new editions in the South.

SANDLER IMPORTS, Sausalito, CA
Sales Coordinator, 1998–2002
• Managed seven field representatives.
• Handled information dissemination and distribution.
• Codesigned a full-color catalog.
• Placed advertising in major trade publications.
• Promoted products at trade shows.

REDWOOD PUBLISHING CO., San Francisco, CA
Distribution Assistant, 1993–1998
• Developed new distribution outlets.
• Increased distribution in district by 25 percent over two years.

EDUCATION
Miami University, Miami, OH
B.S. in Communications, 1993

PROFESSIONAL MEMBERSHIPS
Sausalito Community Association
San Francisco Chamber of Commerce
American Publishing Association

SEMINARS
"Publishing in Modern Times," Chicago, IL
"International Publishing," New York, NY

REFERENCES
Available on request.

YOSHEMA MUNO

7640 North Redden Road • Eugene, OR 78221

Y.Muno@xxx.com • (330) 555-2300

JOB OBJECTIVE

A management position for a quality shoe and accessory store.

EXPERIENCE

Florsheim Shoes, Eugene, OR

Assistant Manager, 2003 to Present

- Serve as assistant manager of a quality shoe store.
- Partially responsible for supervision of eight salespeople.
- Research customers' buying habits and preferences.
- Handle promotion and mailings for sales and in-store events.
- Increase sales through personal attention to customer's needs.

Handleman Shoe Store, Eugene, OR

Salesperson, 1999 to 2003

- Sold high-quality women's shoes at an exclusive store.
- Named top salesperson of 2002 and 2003.
- Maintained a clean, attractive store and organized inventory.

Born Shoes, Portland, OR

Salesperson, 1996 to 1999

- Assisted customers in making purchase decisions.
- Organized and maintained stock and delivery.
- Designed window displays.

EDUCATION

Stevenson Community College, Portland, OR

Associate's in Business, 1996 to 1998

Calumet High School, Calumet, IL

Graduated 1996

REFERENCES

Available on request.

THEODORE WELLINGTON

34 WASHINGTON DRIVE
NEW YORK, NY 10019
TED.WELLINGTON@XXX.NET
(212) 555-4904

JOB OBJECTIVE
A senior management position in sales and marketing.

ACHIEVEMENTS
- Introduced new and existing product line through presentations to marketing directors.
- Developed new product that resulted in increased sales.
- Quadrupled sales during the past five years.
- Supervised seven sales agencies throughout the United States and Canada.
- Developed 17 new accounts.
- Researched the market in order to coordinate product line with current trends.

EMPLOYMENT HISTORY
Surf City Skateboard Company, New York, NY
Vice President of Sales and Marketing, 1999–Present

Nike, Inc., San Jose, CA
Sales and Marketing Manager, 1994–1999

Vans, Ltd., Los Angeles, CA
Sales Representative, 1989–1994

EDUCATION
University of Southern California, Los Angeles, CA
B.S. in Marketing, 1989

SEMINARS
Manhattan Sales and Marketing Seminar, 2000, 2001
National Marketing Association Conference, 2001–2004

REFERENCES
Provided on request.

DAREN TREVOL

4343 Wild Rose Way

Santa Fe, NM 88005

Darentrevol@xxx.com

(909) 555-4328

OBJECTIVE
Senior Vice President of Sales and Marketing for Vincent Electronics, Incorporated.

ACHIEVEMENTS
MARKETING
- Researched computer market to coordinate product line with current tastes and buying trends.
- Developed new approaches to marketing software products, including in-store displays and advertising.
- Organized and planned convention displays and strategies.

SALES
- Introduced new and existing product lines through presentations to major clients.
- Increased sales from $12 million to $38 million in four years.
- Developed nine new accounts.
- Supervised five sales agencies nationwide.

WORK HISTORY
Vincent Electronics, Inc., Santa Fe, NM
Sales and Marketing Manager, 2000 to Present

Porcelana Inc., Portales, NM
Product Coordinator, 1995 to 2000

Radio Shack, Inc., Las Cruces, NM
Sales Representative, 1990 to 1995

EDUCATION
Eastern New Mexico University, Portales, NM
Bachelor of Science, 1990
Major: Business Administration
Minor: Computer Science

REFERENCES
Available on request.

JOHN L. RYDER
211 W. Timberline Rd.
Boulder, CO 80301
jryder@xxx.com
(719) 555-9080

JOB OBJECTIVE
Seeking a sales management position in a medium- to large-sized insurance company.

ACCOMPLISHMENTS
◆ Increased sales 17 percent in my first year of selling group policies to businesses and unions. Sales increases have averaged 15 percent to 20 percent in subsequent years.
◆ Chaired a committee that developed a sales manual that explained group insurance sales techniques.
◆ Served as insurance adjustor for Brooklyn Health Company, a 20,000-member HMO.
◆ Handled highly technical reimbursements by the state to the HMO.
◆ Wrote and edited quarterly and annual reports.
◆ Investigated and reported on adjustments and claims.

WORK EXPERIENCE
Interco Insurance Company, Boulder, CO
Insurance Agent, 2000–Present

Denver Health Company, Denver, CO
Health Insurance Adjustor, 1995–2000

City of St. Louis, St. Louis, MO
Claims Adjustor, 1990–1995

EDUCATION
M.B.A., Washington University, St. Louis, MO, 1995
B.A., Washington University, St. Louis, MO, 1988

OTHER
Willing to travel and relocate if necessary.

REFERENCES
Available upon request.

THERESA BROWN

12 Church Road
St. Paul, MN 51311
t.brown@xxx.com
(612) 555-6565

JOB OBJECTIVE
A position as a marketing representative for a manufacturer of textiles.

PROFESSIONAL ACHIEVEMENTS
Marketing
Demonstrated the value of quantity purchases to customers.
Researched industry competition to refine selling techniques.
Projected success of new products through surveys and questionnaires.

Sales
Established and maintained an excellent relationship with over 100
accounts in the textile industry.
Resolved customer complaints promptly.
Provided customers with detailed information on product line.
Named Salesperson of the Month six times.

WORK HISTORY
Rand Textiles, Inc., St. Paul, MN
Sales Representative, 4/02-Present

St. Paul Woolen Products, St. Paul, MN
Salesperson, 5/99-3/02

EDUCATION
Pottersville Community College, Pottersville, MN
Majored in Business
Attended, 1997-1999

St. Rose High School, St. Olaf, MN
Graduated, June 1997

REFERENCES
Available upon request.

Kelly McDougall

16 East Mayfair Road
Kearney, NE 68588
K-McDougall@xxx.net
Evening: (308) 555-9339

OBJECTIVE: A sales position in commercial real estate

EXPERIENCE: ERA Realty, Inc., Kearney, NE
Domestic Real Estate Salesperson, 2002 to Present
- Sell homes in the northwest suburban area.
- Interact with clients, real estate agents, brokers, and bank personnel.
- Awarded ERA Northwest Suburban Salesperson of the Year, 2003.

Wolf Camera Shop, Lincoln, NE
Camera Salesperson, 1999 to 2002
- Sold cameras and film.
- Assisted customers in filling orders and making repairs.
- Trained new members of sales staff.
- Reorganized inventory system.

ACTIVITIES: Member, Northwest Suburban Realty Association
2002 to Present

EDUCATION: University of Nebraska, Lincoln, NE
B.S. in Business
1999 to 2001

Harper Community College, Omaha, NE
1998 to 1999

SKILLS:
- Proficient in Microsoft Word, Excel, and PowerPoint
- Background with customized databases and graphs
- Knowledge of a variety of online research resources
- Experience with public speaking and making sales presentations

REFERENCES: Provided upon request

ADILA HUSAK
12677 Telegraph Road
Dearborn, MI 48066
A.Husak@xxx.com
(810) 555-2343

JOB OBJECTIVE

A management position in cable television advertising sales.

EXPERIENCE

- Sold space in television for four major clients in the automotive industry.
- Served as a liaison between clients and television and radio station salespeople.
- Researched demographic and public buying habits for clients.
- Sold space for daytime programming on local television station.
- Advised station on content and suitability of ads.
- Served as a liaison between station and those purchasing advertising space.

EMPLOYMENT HISTORY

Medialink Advertising Agency, Detroit, MI
Television Space Sales, September 2000–Present

KTUT Television, Auburn Hills, MI
Television Space Sales, October 1998–August 2000

KFTF Radio, Berkeley, CA
Staff Sales Assistant, June 1996–June 1998

EDUCATION

University of California at Berkeley
B.A. in Communications, 1998

HONORS

Seeger Award, Outstanding Communications Senior, 1998
Dean's List, five semesters
Salutatorian, Overland High School, Palo Alto, CA, 1994

REFERENCES ON REQUEST

POLLY LOPEZ

8909 S. Alvira St. • Los Angeles, CA 90028 • P.Lopez@xxx.com • (904) 555-9090

OBJECTIVE

To obtain a position in market research where I can focus on needs/trends analysis, demographics, and market surveys.

WORK EXPERIENCE

Southern California Tours, Inc., Los Angeles, CA
Research Analyst Assistant, 2002 to Present

- Project sales potential by interpreting sales figures from yearly data.
- Develop target campaigns that increase the efficiency of company's direct-mail approach.
- Analyze incoming market data on customers for demographic purposes.
- Initiate changes in marketing strategy that improve customer satisfaction.

American Hospital Supply Corporation, San Diego, CA
Sales Assistant, 1998 to 2002

- Researched and wrote training bulletins on communication and sales strategy for the sales staff.
- Trained new salespeople.
- Prepared proposals for the regional sales manager.
- Handled scheduling and travel arrangements for the sales department.
- Planned and executed all special events.

EDUCATION

University of California, La Jolla, CA
B.A. in English, 1998
Graduated with honors in English
Dean's List, 1997, 1998

ACTIVITIES

President, Senior Writing Club, 1998
Captain, Women's Tennis Team, 1997 to 1998

SPECIAL SKILLS

Working knowledge of Spanish and French.
Extensive experience with design and layout software, including Quark, Page-Maker, and Photoshop.

References furnished upon request.

DIAGO VASQUEZ

65 West Harrison Street
Minneapolis, MN 44490
DiagoVasquez@xxx.com
(612) 555-2901

JOB OBJECTIVE

Sales manager for a computer software manufacturer

PROFESSIONAL EXPERIENCE

Sales and Promotion
Made cold calls and visits to software retailers that resulted in increased accounts.
Visited and serviced existing accounts to encourage continued sales.
Advised customers on options available to meet a wide range of product needs.
Handled dealer requests for information and sample products.

Marketing
Researched competitive products to evaluate competitors' strengths and weaknesses.
Planned a marketing strategy that resulted in 20 percent increase in accounts.
Maintained demographic data in order to ascertain buyer profiles.

EMPLOYMENT HISTORY

Thomas Software Inc., Minneapolis, MN
Assistant Sales Manager, 2000–Present
Sales Representative, 1998–2000

Quaker & Company, St. Paul, MN
Marketing Assistant, 1997–1998

USE Computer Sales, St. Paul, MN
Salesperson, 1995–1997

Bennigan's Restaurant, St. Paul, MN
Waiter, 1994–1995

Page 1 of 2

EDUCATION

Concordia University, St. Paul, MN
B.A. in Marketing, 1997

HONORS

Phi Beta Kappa, 1997
Dean's List, 1995–1997
Terrance C. Maples Marketing Scholarship Recipient, 1995–1996
President, Student Activities Board, 1997

COMPUTER KNOWLEDGE

Both Mac and PC operating systems
Entire Microsoft Office Suite, including Excel, PowerPoint, and Photoshop
Web editing software, including FrontPage
Layout software, including PageMaker and Publisher

REFERENCES

Provided on request

MARIA CRUCIANO

5555 Euclid Avenue
Ft. Lauderdale, FL 33053
M.Cruciano@xxx.com
(305) 555-6001

OBJECTIVE
A sales management position with a machine tool manufacturer where I can apply my abilities and experience in sales and marketing.

WORK EXPERIENCE
Florida Hydraulics, Inc., Miami, FL
Assistant Sales Manager, January 2000–Present
Manage a staff of seven sales representatives. Supervise the production of a marketing newsletter that has circulation throughout the company. Cowrite the annual marketing plan. Serve as a liaison between sales staff and upper management.

Peston Machine Tools, Inc., Tampa, FL
Sales Representative, March 1997–November 1999
Sold machine tools to business and industry. Wrote articles on sales techniques for monthly newsletter. Handled seven accounts in which sales rose 29 percent during my tenure.

EDUCATION
B.S. in Civil Engineering
University of Miami, Miami, FL
August 1996

AFFILIATIONS
Machine Tools Sales Organization, Melbourne, FL
1999–Present

Society of Civil Engineers, New York, NY
1998–Present

SKILLS
Fluent in Italian.

REFERENCES
Available on request.

CAROL A. BADEN

Permanent Address:
12 East Hollow Road
Berlin, NY 10951
(518) 555-6057
C-Baden@xxx.com

Temporary Address:
150 Fort Washington Avenue
New York, NY 10032
(212) 555-4959

OBJECTIVE:
A sales trainee position with a financial planning group.

EDUCATION:
New York University, New York, NY
B.S., Communications, May 2005
Minor: Economics
Communications GPA: 3.6
Academic GPA: 3.5

EXPERIENCE:
V.I.T.A. (Volunteer Income Tax Assistance), Spring 2004
• Provided income tax assistance to lower income and elderly taxpayers who were unable to prepare returns or pay for professional assistance.

Tutor, Economics Department, New York University, 2004
• Helped students to better understand basic concepts in the study of Economics.

Salesperson, Parker's Department Store, Summer, 2002
• Assisted customers with all aspects of purchases. Responsible for cash management, inventory, and displays.

Clerical Assistant, Order Department, Castle Catering, 2001
• Took phone orders.
• Assisted with bookkeeping.

HONORS:
Senior Service Award, New York University, 2004
Dean's List, Fall 2004 and Spring 2005

SKILLS:
Comfortable with public speaking.
Extensive background with computers.
Familiar with current tax and financial regulations.

REFERENCES:
Available upon request.

★ JASMINE PEHOWSKI

5 E. Randall Rd.
Providence, RI 00898
jpehowski@xxx.com
(401) 555-6768

GOAL
Assistant Sales Manager position

WORK HISTORY
Sales Representative, 2000–Present, American Telecom, Providence, RI
★ Identify customer needs and problems and provide personalized
   service.
★ Identify potential new customers and establish new accounts.
★ Increased client base by 30 percent during tenure.
★ Prepare sales forecasts and sales reports.
★ Coordinate with the marketing and research teams to develop
   presentations.

Sales Representative, 1997–2000, Amadala Foods, Inc., Boston, MA
★ Orchestrated market analyses and researched competition for reports
   to the district manager.
★ Developed monthly sales plans that identified necessary account
   maintenance and specific problems that required attention.
★ Resolved service and billing problems.
★ Maintained daily sales logs and referral logs.

Salesperson, 1992–1997, Century 21 Realty, Cambridge, MA
★ Sold homes in the Cambridge area.
★ Interacted and coordinated with clients, real estate agents, brokers,
   and bank personnel.
★ Awarded Salesperson of the Year award three times.

EDUCATION
B.A. in Business, 1991
Cambridge College, Cambridge, MA
Received Harriet Johnson Business Scholarship.

SKILLS
Proficient in Word, PowerPoint, and Excel.

REFERENCES
Available upon request.

LUIS CONTRARO

12 Derbyshire Drive
East St. Louis, IL 60989
L.Contraro@xxx.net
(314) 555-8932

JOB SOUGHT

A position as manager of the electronics department of a major retail store

WORK EXPERIENCE

Bergstrom's, St. Louis, MO

Assistant Manager, 2001–Present
Salesperson, 1999–2001
Customer Service Representative, 1998–1999
- Promoted from customer service representative to salesperson and then to assistant manager of electronics at Bergstrom's.
- Currently manage a staff of four.
- Responsible for hiring, training new staff, and supervision.
- Oversee inventory and order from wholesale companies.
- Assist customers in choosing electronic products and designing entertainment centers.

Radio Shack, East St. Louis, IL

Salesperson, Summers, 1996–1998
- Sold electronic products and equipment.
- Handled inventory and product orders.
- Assisted customers with technical questions.

EDUCATION

Barton Community College, St. Louis, MO

Attended, 1998
- Courses included Sales Techniques and Retail Management

East St. Louis High School, East St. Louis, IL

Graduated, June 1998
- Top 10 percent of class
- Student Council President
- Member, Latino Students' Alliance

REFERENCES

Provided on request

GINA STEVENSON

433 East Pointe Road
Ruston, LA 70404
Gina.Stevenson@xxx.com
(985) 555-2341

OBJECTIVE
To become part of the sales and marketing team at Laura Ashley, Inc.

WORK EXPERIENCE
Gina Designs, Ruston, LA
Owner/Designer, 1996 to Present

Established a national market for my original clothing line. Display and merchandise clothing items at retail stores and fashion shows. Increased sales 300 percent in the past two years. Order supplies, process purchase orders and invoices, and ship products.

Tillman's Inc., New Orleans, LA
Assistant Sales Manager, 1995 to 1996

Sold clothing and gifts at the retail level. Ordered stock and maintained inventory. Increased sales by developing in-store promotion program.

Lynn's Hallmark, New Orleans, LA
Manager, 1990 to 1995
Salesperson, 1985 to 1990

Managed gift shop and supervised ten employees. Maintained inventory, sales records, and bank deposits. Ordered products, processed purchase orders and invoices, and handled all payroll duties. Sold gift items.

EDUCATION
B.A., Interior Design, 1990
Xavier University, New Orleans, LA

REFERENCES
Provided on request.

JAMES KENDALL

6678 W. Ridgeway • Omaha, NE 68504 • J.Kendall@xxx.com • (402) 555-7779

PROFESSIONAL OBJECTIVE

Sales position with a dynamic brokerage house.

EXPERIENCE

JONES & JONES, Omaha, NE
Commodity Broker, 1998 to Present
Handle more than 500 clients as a specialist in corn and wheat futures.
Provide written market forecasts to salespeople.
Publish and distribute a weekly newsletter on futures.

KAREN SCHWARTZ, INC., Omaha, NE
Commodity Sales, 1995 to 1998
Managed a client list of more than 300.
Researched and wrote in-house reports on wheat market forecasts.
Named Salesperson of the Year, 1996.

PICKERING, PICKERING & GOLD, Jefferson City, MO
Commodity Trader, 1990 to 1995
Traded cattle futures in-pit on the Chicago Commodities Exchange.

EDUCATION

B.A., Economics, 1990
Nebraska Wesleyan University, Lincoln, NE
Minor: English

PROFESSIONAL MEMBERSHIPS

American Society of Commodities Brokers
New York Business Alliance

SEMINARS

"Commodity Futures," University of Wisconsin, Madison, 1999

REFERENCES

Available

JOANNA P. DOBSON

5660 West Seventh Street
Des Moines, IA 50399
Cellular: 515-555-3453
J.Dobson@xxx.com

OBJECTIVE

To be placed in a marketing research position where I can assist in the development of sales and marketing strategies for a major medical supplies company.

ACHIEVEMENTS

- Developed and implemented marketing strategies for a major manufacturer of disposable medical supplies sold for the purposes of anesthesia administration, IV therapy, and open-heart surgery.
- Served as a research and development specialist for a surgical supply manufacturer. Often worked directly with doctors during procedures in the operating and recovery rooms.
- Managed a five-state sales area on the East Coast. Increased sales by 38 percent during my three-year tenure as a surgical supplies representative. Increased number of clients by 27 percent, which led to a significant increase in revenue.
- Started a personal website (DobsonMedicalBoard) with a message board to discuss medical equipment with doctors. Began marketing products through e-mail to keep contact with busy doctors and save travel time.

WORK EXPERIENCE

Americon, Inc., Des Moines, IA
Marketing Coordinator, 2002 to Present

Meico Surgical Company, Des Moines, IA
Research and Development Specialist, 2000 to 2002

U.S. Medical, Harrisburg, PA
Sales Representative, 1998 to 2000

EDUCATION

B.S., Biology, 1998
University of Pennsylvania
Graduated in top 10 percent of class

REFERENCES

Available on request.

GERALD ROBERT SCAMPI

499 W. 57th St.
New York, NY 10019
G_Scampi@xxx.com
(212) 555-3678

JOB OBJECTIVE
Vice President of Promotion for a communications company.

PROFESSIONAL EXPERIENCE
ATLANTIC RECORDS, New York, NY
Promotion Manager, 2001-Present
Develop and execute all marketing strategies for record promotion in
New York, New Jersey, and Massachusetts. Interface with sales department
and retail stores to ensure adequate product placement. Attend various
company-sponsored sales, marketing, and management seminars.

RSO RECORDS, Miami, FL
Promotion Manager, 1993-2001
Planned all marketing strategies for record promotions in the southeast
United States. Worked closely with sales and touring bands to
ensure product visibility in the marketplace.

WCFL RADIO, Chicago, IL
On-Air Personality, 1990-1992
Played CHR music. Made TV appearances and public-events appearances
for the station. Organized and staffed station's news department.
Promoted to Music Director after one year.

WGLT RADIO, Atlanta, GA
Program Director, Music Director, and News Director, 1985-1990
Outlined daily news and music program for morning segment.
Bought advertising to increase sales. Directed publicity campaign.

EDUCATION
COLUMBIA COLLEGE, Chicago, IL
Attended 1984-1985.
Studied Audio Engineering.

REFERENCES AVAILABLE

INGVAR T. KOPESKI

501 West Glendale Boulevard   I.Kopeski@xxx.com
Kansas City, MO 51132   (816) 555-9090

Objective
Regional sales manager position for a national pharmaceutical manufacturer/
distributor.

Experience
RFB Pharmaceuticals, Kansas City, MO
District Sales Manager, 1999-Present
- Direct the selling and servicing of accounts to physicians, pharmacies, and
  hospitals in the Kansas City area.
- Increased sales by 50 percent during the last four years.
- Initiated an incentive plan that resulted in 21 new accounts.
- Worked with production department to improve product quality.

Jacobs & Jacobs Advertising, Trenton, NJ
Display Coordinator, 1996-1999
- Coordinated and supervised the installation of displays in men's clothing
  stores in the Trenton area.
- Supervised a seven-person office in all aspects of display planning and
  production.
- Worked to help place the firm in the syndicated display advertising field.

Mark Shale, Inc., Schaumburg, IL
Retail Store Manager, 1992-1996
- Promoted from salesperson to assistant manager to manager within two
  years.
- Supervised the designing of displays for interior and windows.
- Handled all aspects of personnel, sales promotions, inventory control, and
  new products.
- Interacted with corporate management frequently.

Education
American Institute, Putnum, NJ
Completed course on Sales Techniques, 1998

Harper College, Palatine, IL
Attended 1990-1992
Majored in Advertising

Page 1 of 2

Memberships
Kansas City Sales Association
Member, 1999-Present

Kansas City Community Development Association
Member, 1999-Present
Cochair, Community Fund-raising Project

American Display Advertisers, 1996-1999
Treasurer, 1997

Awards
Community Service Certificate, 2002
Kansas City Chamber of Commerce

Salesperson of the Year, 1993
Mark Shale Corporation

Excellence in Advertising Award, 1998
American Display Advertisers

References
On request.

Sarah Jung

1800 West Third St • Modesto, CA 98088
sarahjung@xxx.com • (415) 555-9202

Objective

A management position in sales and marketing.

Professional Experience

Rolex Watches, Inc., San Francisco, CA
Vice President of Sales and Marketing, 1994-Present
➤ Increased watch sales by $30 million during the past three years.
➤ Introduced new and existing product lines through presentations to marketing directors throughout the United States and Canada.
➤ Developed new products expanding from watches to other accessories, which resulted in increased sales.
➤ Increased company's share through innovation and improved quality.

Peters and Company, Salt Lake City, UT
District Sales Manager, 1989-1994
➤ Planned successful strategies to develop new accounts.
➤ Increased sales by at least 25 percent each year.
➤ Researched and analyzed market conditions in order to expand customer base.
➤ Developed weekly and monthly sales goals and strategies.
➤ Supervised seven sales representatives.

Herzz, Inc., Los Angeles, CA
Sales Representative, 1984-1989
➤ Developed and managed new territories.
➤ Built sales through calls on retailers and wholesalers.
➤ Developed creative techniques for increasing product sales.
➤ Maintained current knowledge of competitive products.
➤ Wrote weekly and monthly sales reports.

Education

University of Southern California, Los Angeles, CA
B.S. in Marketing, 1983

Seminars

Southern California Marketing Seminar, 2002-2003
National Retailers' Association, 1997-2001

References available.

CHRISTOPHER SMALLS

600 West Porter Street, #5
Las Vegas, NV 89890
Chris.Smalls@xxx.com
(514) 555-3893

OBJECTIVE

A position as a marketing trainee in a manufacturing company.

EDUCATION

University of Nevada, Las Vegas, NV
Bachelor of Science in Business
Expected June 2005

HONORS

- Dean's List for four semesters.
- Dornburn Scholarship.
- University of Nevada Undergraduate Business Award.

WORK EXPERIENCE

Porter Rand & Associates, Seattle, WA
Sales Intern, 2004
- Assisted sales staff in the areas of sales forecasts, identifying new customers, and promotion.

University of Nevada, Las Vegas, NV
Research/Office Assistant, 2002-2003
- Researched and compiled materials for department professors.
- Arranged filing system and supervisor's library.
- Organized department inventory.

SPECIAL SKILLS

- Experience using Mac and PC operating systems.
- Familiar with multiple layout, design, database, and e-mail programs.
- Confident learning new technology.
- Digital photography background.
- Knowledge of *Associated Press Stylebook* and *The Chicago Manual of Style*.

References furnished upon request.

DAVID P. JENKINS

365 Wealthy Street, Apt. 1
Grand Rapids, MI 49505
DP.Jenkins@xxx.com
(616) 555-3472

JOB OBJECTIVE

A position as a sales/marketing manager where I can utilize my knowledge and experience by combining high-volume selling of major accounts with an administrative ability that increases sales through encouragement of sales team.

EMPLOYMENT HISTORY

TRIBOR INDUSTRIES, Holland, MI
Regional Sales Manager, 2000-Present
Manage sales of all product lines in western markets. Represent four corporate divisions with combined annual sales of approximately $3 million. Direct and motivate a sales force of 12 in planned selling to achieve company goals.

TRIBOR INDUSTRIES, Holland, MI
District Manager, 1995-2000
Acted as district sales manager for the Grand Rapids metropolitan area. Built up wholesale and dealer distribution substantially over a five-year period, culminating in promotion to regional sales manager.

AMERICAN OFFICE SUPPLY, Rockford, MI
Assistant to Sales Manager, 1991-1995
Handled both internal and external areas of sales and marketing. Served as company sales representative and sold a variety of office supplies to retail outlets.

EDUCATION

University of Michigan, Ann Arbor, MI
B.A. in Business Administration, 1991
Major: Management

SEMINARS
National Management Association Seminar, 2000
"Sales Strategies 2000"

Greater Grand Rapids Business Institute Seminars, 1998-2003
"Motivating Experienced Sales Staff"
"Advanced Direct Marketing Techniques"

HONORS
Manager of the Year
Tribor Industries, 2002

Top Monthly Sales, five times
American Office Supply, 1991-1995

REFERENCES
Provided upon request.

SARA STEVENS

332 East Geobert Road
Terre Haute, IN 48930
S.Stevens@xxx.net
(317) 555-3890

Goal

To manage a floral shop.

Work History

Terry's Flowers, Terre Haute, IN
Assistant Sales Manager, 1999-Present
- Sell flowers, wait on customers, fill phone orders, handle special orders, and design window displays.
- Place ads for special promotions.
- Represent store at sales conventions.

Avant Books, Indianapolis, IN
Salesperson, 1998-1999
- Sold books to customers, filled special orders, and arranged inventory.
- Handled customer returns and special requests.

Education

Revers High School, Indianapolis, IN
Graduated June 1998
Ranked 15 in class of 250.
Worked in student bookstore for three years.

References

Available on request.

CAROLINE DONAGHY

15001 Irvine Meadows Drive • Calistoga, FL 28088
C.Donaghy@xxx.com • (305) 555-8398

OBJECTIVE

A management-level sales position.

EMPLOYMENT HISTORY

Simpco, Inc., Tampa, FL
Regional Sales Manager, 1998 to Present
• Manage sales of all product lines in southern markets for a leading
  manufacturer of fixtures.
• Represent five corporate divisions of the company, with sales in
  excess of $2 million annually.
• Direct and motivate twelve sales representatives in planned selling to
  achieve company goals.

Lucky Industries, Miami, FL
District Manager, 1993 to 1998
• Acted as sales representative for the Miami metropolitan area.
• Built both wholesale and dealer distribution substantially during
  my tenure.
• Developed monthly sales plans that identified specific problems that
  required attention.

National Office Products, Inc., Baton Rouge, LA
Assistant Sales Manager, 1984 to 1993
• Handled both internal and external areas of sales and marketing,
  including samples, advertising, and pricing.
• Served as company sales representative and sold a variety of office
  supplies to retail stores.

EDUCATION

Southeastern Louisiana University, Hammond, LA
B.A. in English, 1984

SEMINARS

American Sales Association Seminars, 2000 to 2003

REFERENCES

Available on request.

JANIS DARIEN

345 West Third Street, #42
Boston, MA 02210
janisdarien@xxx.com
(617) 555-3291

JOB OBJECTIVE

To obtain a position as a marketing management trainee.

EDUCATION

B.A. degree in Economics, June 2003
Boston University, Boston, MA
Dean's list five quarters
3.8 GPA

- Plan to pursue graduate studies toward a Master's degree in Marketing in an evening program.

WORK EXPERIENCE

Lewis Advertising Agency, Boston, MA
Marketing Assistant, September 2003 to Present
- Assist Marketing Manager in areas of promotion, product development, and demographic analysis.

Paterno Marketing, Boston, MA
Telephone Interviewer, Summer 2004
- Conducted telemarketing surveys to help clients analyze demographics and product demand and create marketing strategies.

SPECIAL SKILLS

Fluent in French.
Proficient with entire Microsoft Office Suite.
Background with online research.

REFERENCES

Available on request.

MICHAEL BAHIRINI

4420 Conifer Mt. Rd.
Denver, CO 80433
M-Bahirini@xxx.com
(303) 555-9098

JOB SOUGHT:

Promotion Director for a television station

*SKILLS AND
ACHIEVEMENTS:*

Promotion/Marketing
Wrote and designed promotional pieces
- Evaluated content and direction of promotions
- Handled market research/demographic research
- Consulted clients on marketing plans

Video Production
- Handled shooting procedures, audio, lighting, casting, and editing
- Wrote and edited shooting scripts
- Determined production values for marketing accounts
- Oversaw postproduction and placement

Media Planning
Advised clients on media strategies
- Oversaw media budgets
- Determined and implemented marketing objectives
- Negotiated spot rates for clients

EMPLOYMENT:

Geary Advertising, Inc., Denver, CO
Media Planner, 2002 to present

Goebert & Radner, Inc., Dillon, CO
Assistant Media Buyer, 1999 to 2002

Sears Inc., Des Moines, IA
Advertising Assistant, 1997 to 1999

EDUCATION:

Drake University, Des Moines, IA
B.A. in Economics, Minor in Advertising
Graduated in 1997
Phi Beta Kappa

REFERENCES:

On request

CHRISTOPHER KNIGHT

1700 W. Armadillo
Mesa, Arizona 88631
Chris.Knight@xxx.com
(619) 555-2839

OBJECTIVE

To obtain a position as Vice President of Public Relations with an aeronautical corporation.

AREAS OF EXPERIENCE

Marketing Development

- Initiated and supervised sales programs for aircraft distributors selling aircraft to businesses throughout the western United States.
- Managed accounts with a profit range of $100,000 to $1,000,000, including Dow Chemical, Landston Steel, Mercury Company, Berkeley Metallurgical, and Ford Motor Company.
- Demonstrated to customer companies how to use aircraft to coordinate and consolidate expanding facilities.
- Introduced and expanded use of aircraft for musical tours.

Public Relations

- Handled all levels of sales promotion, corporate public relations, and training on company use of aircraft.
- Managed promotions including personal presentations, radio and television broadcasts, news stories, and magazine features.

Pilot Training

- Taught primary, secondary, and instrument flight in single and multiengine aircraft.

EMPLOYMENT HISTORY

Hughes Aircraft, Inc., Mesa, AZ
Sales Manager and Chief Pilot, 2001 to Present

Boeing Corporation, Kansas City, MO
Assistant Manager of Promotion, 1992 to 2001

EMPLOYMENT HISTORY cont'd.

American Airlines, Dallas, TX
Pilot, 1985 to 1992

United States Air Force, Houston, TX
Flight Instructor, 1983 to 1985

PROFESSIONAL LICENSE

Airline Transport Rating 14352-60
Single, Multiengine Land
Flight Instructor—Instrument

EDUCATION

University of Texas, Houston, TX
B.A. in History, 1980

MILITARY SERVICE

United States Air Force
1980 to 1985

REFERENCES

Available on request.

JOHNNY KAZELL

5320 Wilshire Blvd.
Los Angeles, CA 90069
jkazell@xxx.com
(213) 555-9282

OBJECTIVE

Seeking a marketing position in the music industry.

WORK EXPERIENCE

Premier Productions, Los Angeles, CA
Public Relations/Marketing Assistant, 5/02–Present
Assist Public Relations Director with all duties, including radio promotion and retail marketing.
Coordinate radio and print interviews for artists.
Typing, filing, and answering phones.

BMG Online Radio, Los Angeles, CA
Music Director, 6/01–5/02
Selected appropriate music for student radio station.
Oversaw daily operations of music library and programming department.
Supervised staff of six student volunteers.

EDUCATION

University of California–Los Angeles, Los Angeles, CA
B.A. in Arts Management, May 2002

ACTIVITIES

Phi Mu Alpha Music Fraternity, President
Alpha Lambda Fraternity

SPECIAL SKILLS

Proficient with Microsoft Office.
Extensive knowledge of music history and pop culture.
Fluent in Spanish.
Type 55 wpm.

References available on request.

Mohamed Ahmad

1200 Woodler Drive   M.Ahmad@xxx.com
Madison, WI 66534   (853) 555-4903

Objective:	A position as a sales assistant.
Education:	University of Wisconsin, Madison, WI B.A. in Advertising, expected June 2005 Dean's List four quarters 3.6 GPA in major field 3.5 GPA overall
Activities:	Alumni Committee Student Activities Board
Work Experience:	SBC, Madison, WI Sales Intern, September 2004 to Present • Assist sales manager in areas of marketing promotion and product development. HANDELMAN MARKETING, Milwaukee, WI Telephone Surveyor, Summer 2003 YESTERDAY'S, Milwaukee, WI Waiter, Summer 2002
Special Skills:	• Familiar with Word, PowerPoint, and Excel • Knowledge of a variety of online research resources • Fluent in Spanish
References:	Available on request

Jacob Rosenthal
Community Relations/Media Specialist

2950 West Best Road
Raleigh, North Carolina 27695
Rosenthal.Communications@xxx.com
(303) 442-5284

Overview

Self-employed communications professional with extensive experience assisting both private and nonprofit agencies to promote services and maintain a positive image in the community.

Education

North Carolina State University
B.A. in Communications, 1992

Work History

Owner, Rosenthal Communications, 1996 to Present

➤ Manage successful freelance business with clients including the City of Raleigh, Raleigh General Hospital, North Carolina State University, Carleton Community College, and Riverside Amusement Corporation.
➤ Design complete publicity packages to inform community of available services, promote corporate identity, and increase sales.
➤ Write press releases, brochures, ad copy, feature articles, and statements to press.
➤ Produce radio and cable television spots.
➤ Develop concept with client and manage all details while supervising subcontractors as necessary and keeping client abreast of progress.

Community Services Director, North Carolina State University, 1994 to 1996

➤ Directed community outreach programs.
➤ Conducted needs assessments and worked in conjunction with academic faculty and administrative staff to meet the needs of diverse learners.

Work History cont'd.

➢ Created distance learning options and promoted these new programs through local and national media.
➢ Arranged off-site course locations for evening division courses.

Production Assistant, WNC-TV, 1992 to 1994

➢ Assisted in production of wide variety of community access programming, including children's and educational television.
➢ Assisted producers on-site with setups and breakdowns of shoots.
➢ Edited footage.
➢ Produced promotional spots and public service announcements.

References

References and portfolio of work are available for review.

LISA STANSFIELD ▼ ▼ ▼

14 E. Three Penny Rd. ▼ Detroit, MI 33290 ▼ lstanfield.com ▼ (313) 555-3489

OBJECTIVE ▼ ▼ ▼

A management position in public relations where I can utilize my promotion and marketing experience.

WORK EXPERIENCE ▼ ▼ ▼

▼ SEVEN ELEVEN INC., Detroit, MI
Marketing Director, 2000–present
Develop a successful marketing campaign for a convenience store chain. Maintain a positive working relationship with radio and print media. Develop marketing strategies to increase sales at underperforming stores. Run a training program for store managers and staff.

▼ SUPER VACUUM COMPANY, Bloomfield Hills, MI
Marketing Representative, 1996–2000
Demonstrated vacuums in specialty and department stores. Reported customer reactions to manufacturers. Created fliers and advertising to promote products.

▼ EMPIRE CARPET, INC., Chicago, IL
Assistant to Sales Manager, 1991–1996
Handled sales and marketing, including samples, advertising, and pricing. Sold carpeting to retail outlets.

EDUCATION ▼ ▼ ▼

UNIVERSITY OF MICHIGAN, Ann Arbor, MI
B.A., Marketing, 1991

SEMINARS ▼ ▼ ▼

Michigan Marketing Workshop, 2002, 2003
Sales and Marketing Association Seminar, 1998

References available on request.

MAXINE DAVIS

916 Rockport Road
Phoenix, AZ 85016
M.Davis@xxx.com
(602) 555-9136

OBJECTIVE:

Obtain a position as a Marketing Executive at the IDEO Corporation.

WORK HISTORY:

Marketing Manager, 9/96 to Present
Southwest Publishing, Phoenix, AZ
Duties:
- Direct publisher's marketing efforts.
- Responsible for producing catalogs and direct-mail pieces.
- Coordinate with advertising department.
- Track sales histories and design pricing and promotional strategies.
- Hire, train, and supervise sales staff.
- Represent publisher at sales conventions and industry trade shows.
- Liaison to wholesalers and distributors.

Advertising Copywriter, 5/93 to 8/96
Current Communications, Inc., Phoenix, AZ
Duties:
- Produced ad copy and brochures.
- Designed, produced, and distributed direct-mail packages.

Telemarketer, 6/92 to 5/93
TDK Marketing, Dallas, TX
Duties:
- Conducted phone surveys to research consumer preferences and purchase patterns.
- Compiled results and drafted reports.

EDUCATION:

B.S. in Communications, June 1992
University of Arizona

MEMBERSHIPS:

American Marketing Association
National Association of Women in Business

REFERENCES:

Portfolio and complete list of references supplied on request.

JUAN CASTILLO

8155 N. Knox St.
Santa Fe, NM 88003
J.Castillo@xxx.net
(505) 555-3168

JOB OBJECTIVE

Sales position where I can utilize my retail sales,
cash management, and supervisory skills.

WORK EXPERIENCE

Gateway, Inc., Santa Fe, NM
Manager/Salesperson, 11/01–Present
• Manage own jewelry business.
• Sell jewelry at wholesale and retail levels.
• Negotiate prices with customers.
• Handle all finances and bookkeeping.

West Miami Jewelry, Miami, FL
Manager, 1/98–11/01
• Managed all aspects of a retail jewelry store.
• Oversaw all aspects of sales, purchasing, and bookkeeping.
• Supervised two employees.

EDUCATION

Santa Fe Business Institute, Santa Fe, NM
2/02–Present
Major: Business Management

University of Miami, FL
Attended 8/96–1/98
Area of concentration: Business Management

References available on request.

PETER SIMMONS

678 Park Street, #546 • Noblesville, IN 46060 • (219) 555-6042

OBJECTIVE

To obtain an executive position in marketing with an emerging company that is dedicated to a long-term program

EXPERIENCE

Senior Partner, 5/00-Present
DCS SOFTWARE, INC., Noblesville, IN
Contingency Marketing Agency
Designed marketing strategies for local and national companies
Directly responsible for meeting payroll of 25 full-time employees
Improved sales for one company by over 25 percent in a 12-month period
Developed marketing programs for corporations

Regional Sales Manager, 1/99-5/00
BLAUVELT ENGINEERS, New York, NY
Business Communications Systems
Set regional sales record in six months
Procured 10 national accounts
Exceeded company goal for the 1999 fiscal year
Developed sales marketing program for the northwest regional area

Marketing Director, 8/95-1/99
EDWARDS AND KELCEY, Livingston, NJ
Implemented international marketing program
Promoted from sales executive to marketing director
Company's sales increased over 100 percent in a 12-month span
Successful in developing database and reselling to customers directly

EDUCATION

Stevens Institute of Technology, NJ
Bachelor of Arts degree in the area of Technical Marketing Design
May 1995

REFERENCES AVAILABLE

MARK HO

P.O. Box 22 • Boston, Massachusetts 02125 • (617) 555-9876

OBJECTIVE

Key executive position in marketing management or general management.

SUMMARY

Fifteen years of diverse, multidisciplinary management experience with broad-based exposure and expertise in the various facets of marketing, operations, sales, and general management.

Demonstrated ability to profitably expand mature businesses and to manage corporate assets for optimum productivity. Proven analytical, conceptual, and people skills.

EDUCATION

M.B.A. in Marketing, University of Massachusetts, 2000
M.S. in Mathematics, Williams College, 1995
B.S. in Mathematics, Williams College, 1993

EXPERIENCE

CADD Conversion
Vice President and Director of Marketing
2000 to Present
- Reversed the 25 percent decline in unit sales volume in the two-year period preceding employment. Increased unit sales volume 6 percent and total sales revenue 18 percent in the subsequent two-year period.
- Developed marketing strategies to exploit existing product opportunities in present and new markets, i.e., commercial, industrial, institutional, and plan. Strategies focused on an expanded product line with exclusive options and different product features, multiple model selections, and complementary new products.
- Conceptualized and implemented an aggressive product diversification effort. Supplementary HVAC products were acquired on a representation basis and now comprise approximately 50 percent of total sales revenue.

Page 1 of 2

- Established and maintained national sales representation network to market industrial/commercial ceiling fans and air handling, air cleaning, and ventilation equipment.
- Identified and developed private-label accounts in three new markets— agricultural, church, and direct mail—resulting in a 25 percent increase in private-label unit sales volume.

Tectonic Software Systems
Business Development Software
1995 to 1999

- Identified and exploited complementary business opportunities in new but related markets, resulting in a 15 percent increase in special OEM Bales.
- Devised a simplified marketing strategy to upgrade, restructure, and optimize the performance of mature strategic business units.
- Developed comprehensive business assessments relative to participation in high-growth, high-profit consumer and industrial product markets.
- Assumed a leading role in the identification, strategic assessment, and financial analysis of complementary business acquisitions.

Multiframe
Marketing and Product Manager
1993 to 1994

- Created a $25M new market by modifying an existing product to meet specific customer needs in the software system for Macintosh.
- Managed the successful launch of two new "engineered" products for the software industry and eliminated outdated product lines.
- Supervised an innovative and persuasive advertising/sales promotion program to create demand for engineered products at the OEM level and to exploit burgeoning after-market sales opportunities

REFERENCES

Available.

YVONNE CORBIN
33E82 Lincoln Road
Little Rock, AR 72204
(501) 555-4394

GOAL
A marketing/publicity position in the recording industry

WORK HISTORY
PTO Production, Little Rock, AR
Public Relations/Marketing Assistant
Dates: 5/02 to Present
Duties: Assist Public Relations Director with all duties, including radio promotion and retail marketing. Coordinate radio and print interviews for artists. Manage all details of office, including scheduling, record keeping, and document preparation.

National Public Radio, Lincoln, NE
Music Director
Dates: 6/01 to 5/02
Duties: Selected appropriate music for a contemporary jazz format. Oversaw daily operations of music library and programming department. Supervised a staff of six.

EDUCATION
University of Nebraska, Lincoln, NE
B.A. in Arts Management, May 2002
G.P.A. in major: 3.8
Received Ross Hunter Arts Management Scholarship

SKILLS
Fluent in French
Strong computer background, both PC and Mac
Familiar with *The Associated Press Stylebook*

Writing samples and references on request

WINONA T. SIMPSON

420 W. Easterly Ave. • Indianapolis, IN 49091
winonasimpson@xxx.com • (317) 555-1212

OBJECTIVE
A management position in marketing or public relations.

PROFESSIONAL ACHIEVEMENTS

Marketing/Public Relations
- Developed a successful marketing campaign for a video rental chain.
- Initiated and maintained a positive working relationship with online, radio, and print media.
- Implemented marketing strategies to increase sales at less-profitable stores.
- Designed a training program for store managers and staff.

Promotion
- Demonstrated electronic equipment in stereo and department stores.
- Reported customer reactions to manufacturers.
- Designed fliers and advertising to promote products.

EMPLOYMENT HISTORY
Dark Star Video, Inc., Indianapolis, IN
Marketing Director, 1995-Present

Jeron Stereo, Bloomington, IN
Marketing Representative, 1992-1995

Kader Advertising, St. Louis, MO
Public Relations Assistant, 1990-1992

EDUCATION
Washington University, St. Louis, MO
B.S. in Education, 1990

HONORS
Phi Beta Kappa, 1990
Top 5 percent of class
Dean's List

References available.

RITA WESTERBURG

3201 W. ORIOLE ST., APT. 23 • PITTSBURGH, PA 28901
412-555-9302 (HOME) • 412-555-4209 (CELL)

JOB SOUGHT

Public relations director for the marketing division of a major clothing manufacturer.

RELEVANT EXPERIENCE

PUBLIC RELATIONS
• Represented company to clients and retailers in order to present new products.
• Organized and planned fashion shows.
• Wrote customer feedback surveys that identified customers' needs and new options for products.

MANAGEMENT
• Managed seven sales representatives.
• Developed a new national distribution network.
• Oversaw sales and marketing budgets.

DEVELOPMENT
• Created print and television ads.
• Published a newsletter that was distributed to current and potential customers.

EMPLOYMENT HISTORY

Design Plus Clothing, Pittsburgh, PA
National Sales Manager, 2000–present
Account Manager, 1998–2000
Assistant Account Manager, 1997–1998
Personnel Assistant, 1995–1997

EDUCATION

B.A. in English, May 1993
University of Pennsylvania, Harrisburg, PA

SEMINARS

American Marketing Association Seminars, 1997–2003

COMPUTER SKILLS

Word • Excel • PowerPoint • ACT! • Gelco • ADMARC

REFERENCES

Available on request.

DIANNE BROWN

3355 Brookshire Parkway
Bellingham, WA 98523
D.Brown@xxx.com
(360) 555-4948

OBJECTIVE

I hope to utilize my communication, problem-solving, and decision-making skills in a sales and marketing position with opportunities for advancement.

EDUCATION

ITT Business Institute, Associate's degree in Sales and Marketing, June 2002

EXPERIENCE

5/02 to Present
Marketing Assistant
SERVICE SOFTWARE INC.
Develop and implement marketing strategies for software design firm. Assist advertising department with ad copy. Write, edit, and proofread catalog copy and user manuals. Write direct-mail pieces. Maintain databases of client base.

6/00 to 5/02
Executive Secretary
NEW WORLD PACKAGING
Responsible for clerical and receptionist duties for packaging firm. Maintained all office files and records. Wrote correspondence to clients and suppliers. Directed all incoming calls. Provided basic customer service. Coordinated all travel arrangements for management. Maintained monthly expenses and yearly budgets.

SKILLS

Word, Excel, PowerPoint, and Photoshop
Typing speed of 70 wpm
Ten-key calculator by touch
Some knowledge of Spanish

REFERENCES AVAILABLE

ROSA LUCERO
609 Lincoln Road • Houston, Texas 77386 • R.Lucero@xxx.com
(713) 555-1947

OBJECTIVE	Management trainee position dealing with the sales and/or marketing of computer hardware and software.
EDUCATION	Baylor University B.S. in Marketing expected June 2005 Minor in Computer Science with coursework in COBOL, BASIC, RPG II, Pascal, SQL, Perl, and C++. GPA of 4.9/5.0. Work 30+ hours/week with a full class load.
EMPLOYMENT	2002 - Present Computer Lab Assistant, Baylor University • Instruct undergraduates in use of computer hardware and software. • Assistance ranges from word-processing instruction to programming assignments. • Make ID badges for staff and students and issue passwords. • Order computer supplies for eight labs across campus. Summers, 2001 - 2002 Sales Associate, Computer World • Sold computer equipment and software. • Answered customers' questions. • Provided ongoing customer service and training. • Handled sales and returns. • Rectified cash drawers at closing.

REFERENCES AVAILABLE

Julie Rajik

114 Aspen Glen Drive • Hamden, CT 06518 • J.Rajik@xxx.com
(776) 555-9282

Objective

Seeking a publicity/marketing position in the communications industry.

Work Experience

Reckless Inc., Hamden, CT
Marketing Director, 9/01-present
❱ Handle distribution, advertising, and mail-order marketing.
❱ Write biographies and coordinate publicity.
❱ Obtain knowledge regarding domestic and overseas independent
   distribution, buyers for U.S. chain stores, and *Billboard* reporters.

Parker Productions, Hamden, CT
Public Relations/Marketing Assistant, 5/00-9/01
❱ Assisted Public Relations Director with all duties, including online/radio
   promotion and retail marketing.
❱ Coordinated radio and print interviews for artists.
❱ Acted as a liaison between artists and media.
❱ Did typing and filing and answered phones.

Teikyo Post Radio, Waterbury, CT
Music Director, 6/99-5/00
❱ Selected appropriate music for a rock and soul format.
❱ Made recommendations on hiring student volunteers.
❱ Oversaw daily operations of music library and programming department.
❱ Handled yearly budget for department.
❱ Supervised a staff of six.

Education

Teikyo Post University, Waterbury, CT
B.A. in Arts Management, June 1999

Activities

Phi Mu Alpha Music Fraternity, President
National Association of College Activities
Alpha Lambda Fraternity

References available.

SERITA TERESA WOODMAN

4553 N. Alamo Avenue
Dallas, TX 74667
216/555-8908
s.woodman@xxx.com

OBJECTIVE:

Sales representative for a company that markets vacation
    packages.

EXPERIENCE:

American Airlines, Inc., Dallas, TX
Sales Representative, 2000–present
- Sell reservations for domestic flights, hotels, and car rentals.
- Market travel packages through travel agencies.
- Negotiate airline and hotel discounts for customers.
- Devise itineraries and solve customers' travel-related problems.

Salt Lake Travel, Salt Lake City, UT
Travel Agent, 1996–2000
- Handled customer reservations for airlines, hotels, and car rentals.
- Advised customers on competitive travel packages and prices.
- Interacted with all major airlines, hotel chains, and car rental companies.

EDUCATION:

University of Illinois, Urbana, IL
    B.A. in Anthropology, 1996

SPECIAL SKILLS:

- Hands-on experience using most travel-related computer systems
  including Apollo.
- Working knowledge of German, French, and Polish.

REFERENCES:

Available.

Chapter 6

Sample Cover Letters

T his chapter contains sample cover letters for people pursuing a wide variety of jobs and careers in sales and marketing, or who already have experience in this field.

There are many different styles of cover letters in terms of layout, level of formality, and presentation of information. These samples also represent people with varying amounts of education and work experience. Choose one cover letter or borrow elements from several different cover letters to help you construct your own.

JOSEPHINE DIAZ
802 Main Street
Dallas, TX 50118
(972) 555-6999
J.Diaz@xxx.com

May 11, 2005

Ms. Sandra Watt
Human Resources
Porter Sporting Goods, Inc.
133 West York Avenue
Dallas, TX 50116

Dear Ms. Watt:

Is Porter Sporting Goods, Inc. in need of a dedicated, talented sales manager?
If so, please consider the enclosed resume.

I am currently employed as assistant sales manager for Wilson Sporting Goods;
I've been with the company since 2000. My experience in sporting goods sales
includes cold calls and visits to retailers that resulted in increased accounts
for Wilson. In addition, I pride myself on conducting extensive research into
competitors' products in order to create and implement successful marketing
strategies.

My research has included Porter Sporting Goods products, and I am impressed
by their high quality. I have always admired your company's insight and innovation and would like to put my skills to work for you. You will see from my resume
that my time at Wilson has prepared me with many skills that would be a
perfect fit at Porter Sporting Goods.

I will call early next week to determine if an interview is appropriate at this time.
Thank you for considering my credentials.

Sincerely,

Josephine Diaz

March 14, 2004

Hollywood Reporter
Box 1140-H
465 Hollywood Way
Burbank, CA 91505

Dear Recruiter:

I am responding to your ad in *The Hollywood Reporter* of March 14th for a marketing assistant. My resume and salary requirements are enclosed, as you requested.

As my resume indicates, I am a recent graduate of California State University at Northridge, where I received a B.A. in Business. My work experience includes an internship at Warner Bros. Studios in Burbank, working in the market research department. The skills and knowledge I gained during my time there have prepared me for a position such as this one.

I know that your marketing staff could make good use of my current skills, and I would consider it a privilege to join an organization with such high standing in the entertainment industry.

If you wish to schedule an interview, you can reach me at 213-555-7649 between 8:00 and 4:00. You may also phone me at my home number, 213-555-3333. Thank you for your time and consideration.

Sincerely,

Ken Phillips
2233 Effingham Place
Los Angeles, CA 90027
kenphillips@xxx.com

Terrell Washington
1723 Irving Park Road
Chicago, IL 60625
twashington@xxx.com
(773) 555-8928

January 21, 2005

Joe Perlman
Sales Manager
Shasta, Inc.
45 East Huron Street
Chicago, IL 60623

Dear Mr. Perlman:

The notice you placed on the company bulletin board for a sales coordinator seems to describe my skills and experience exactly. Therefore, I would like to formally apply for the position.

As you know, I have been working at Shasta for the last three years as a sales representative. My responsibilities have included selling our products to retail outlets, handling customer requests, and training new sales staff. Working at Shasta has been a challenge; I've learned a great deal and feel well qualified to take the next step in my career by becoming the new sales coordinator.

I would like to set up an interview at your convenience. You can reach me at extension 4222 or at home at 773-555-8928. I look forward to hearing from you regarding this opportunity.

Sincerely,

Terrell Washington

JANIS DARIEN

345 West Third Street, #42
Boston, MA 02210
janisdarien@xxx.com
(617) 555-3291

December 11, 2003

David DuPage
Randolph & Associates
1005 South Holland Street
Milwaukee, WI 68411

Dear Mr. DuPage:

I am responding to your job listing for a marketing management trainee that was posted in the placement office at Boston University. My resume is enclosed.

I recently graduated from Boston University with a degree in Economics, and I am anxious to find a position in marketing. Eventually, I plan to continue my education, by working toward a Master's degree in Marketing during the evenings.

My work experience includes my current marketing assistant position for Lewis Advertising Agency in Boston, where I have been able to put my education to use and gain valuable hands-on experience. I was also employed as a telephone interviewer for Paterno Marketing.

I will be in the Milwaukee area the week of the 20th. Would it be possible to set up an interview with you during that week? If so, please contact me at (617) 555-3291.

Thanks for your time and consideration.

Sincerely,

Janis Darien

JAMES KENDALL

6678 W. Ridgeway • Omaha, NE 68504 • J.Kendall@xxx.com • (402) 555-7779

May 24, 2005

Paterson and Company
673 State Road
Jefferson City, MO 33241
Attn: David Snowheart

Dear Mr. Snowheart:

A fellow broker at Jones & Jones recently informed me that you have an opening on your staff for a commodity broker. Therefore I have taken the liberty of sending my resume for consideration.

I have been in the commodities business for the past fifteen years. During that time, I gained experience as a trader, a sales representative, and finally as a broker for Jones & Jones in Omaha. I currently handle more than 500 clients as a specialist in corn and wheat futures. I also publish and distribute a weekly newsletter on futures.

In the early 1990s, I worked for Pickering, Pickering & Gold in Jefferson City and I am looking to relocate back to the area.

I will be in Jefferson City early next month and would be glad to meet with you to discuss this job opening in greater detail. I am most easily reached between 9 and 11 at (402) 555-9809, or feel free to phone me at home in the evening at (402) 555-7779 if that is more convenient. Thank you in advance for your time and consideration.

Sincerely,

James Kendall

JEREMY HOEFNER

1441 Gilbert Street • Providence, RI 00231
Jeremy.Hoefner@xxx.com • (401) 555-3782

June 2, 2005

Silver Publishing Inc.
16735 Vine Street
Kalamazoo, MI 48303
Attn: Delores Darnell, Director of Personnel

Dear Ms. Darnell:

Through your recent press release, I became aware of the departure of Silver's Senior VP of Marketing, Myron Strickland. With that in mind, I am forwarding my resume to you for consideration for the position of Senior Vice President of Marketing.

With more than twenty years of experience in the publishing industry, including my most recent position as Vice President of Marketing at Johnson Publishing in Providence, I feel that I have the experience and the industry knowledge to tackle this challenge. My employment history also includes stints with Rebus Publishing and *Time* Magazine. Please review the attached resume for a detailed look at my marketing and supervisory skills.

I believe that Silver Publishing is a company with a future, and I am convinced that I can help shape and influence that future. I expect great things from myself and from Silver Publishing.

I will be following up this letter with a telephone call next week. I will be in Michigan during the week of June 20th and would be happy to meet with you regarding this position at that time.

Thank you for your kind consideration.

Sincerely,

Jeremy Hoefner

HARRIET SCHUMACHER
1414 Mountain Drive • Bozeman, MT 59715
H.Schumacher@xxx.com • (415) 555-4930

Dana Jacobs
AT&T, Human Resources
5281 Prospect Drive
Portland, OR 97201

Dear Mr. Jacobs:

David Sanderson, the marketing director of AT&T, suggested that I contact
you regarding a possible management trainee position in your sales department. I am enclosing my resume for your consideration.

I will be graduated this month from Montana State University with a degree
in Communications. I was recently inducted into the Communications Honor
Society (Beta Alpha Psi), and I am a member of the Association for International Business (A.I.S.E.C.).

AT&T would be an excellent place for me to begin my career in the communications industry, and I would bring a strong academic background and
work ethic to the position of management trainee.

I will call early next week to follow up on this letter. Please feel free to call
Mr. Sanderson for a reference; he can be reached at (831) 555-2183, x43.
Thank you in advance for your consideration.

Sincerely,

Harriet Schumacher

May 15, 2005

Deborah Klugh
Director of Human Resources
NBC
1220 Rockefeller Plaza
New York, NY 10019

Dear Ms. Klugh:

This letter is in response to your ad in the *New York Times* for a sales assistant.
Per your request, my resume and salary requirements are enclosed.

Next month I will graduate from Boston University with a degree in Business
Administration and a concentration in Sales Management. I was inducted into
Phi Beta Kappa this month and expect to graduate with honors in June.

I am interested in working in the television industry in a sales capacity and would
be pleased to be part of the NBC team. As you will see, my strong academic
background, internship experience, and professional affiliations have prepared
me to begin a career in the television industry.

I would enjoy presenting my qualifications and portfolio in person, and I am
willing to travel to New York for an interview. Meanwhile, thank you for your time
and consideration.

Sincerely,

Omar Saleh
Boston University
Fenton Hall
199 West Hampshire Way
Boston, MA 02201
(612) 555-3839

Terrell Johnson

3240 Spring Road
Clarksville, AR 72204
T.Johnson@xxx.com
(213) 555-9832

June 11, 2005

David G. Sandler
Director of Human Resources
Nessex Motor Company
1200 Whitting Blvd.
Little Rock, AR 72201

Dear Mr. Sandler:

I am writing in response to the ad in last Sunday's *Arkansas Democrat-Gazette* regarding the opening for the position of assistant manager at the Nessex dealership in Santa Fe.

Currently, I am a sales representative for Yugo in Eureka Springs. My duties there, besides sales, include market analyses, research, forecasts, and resolution of sales and billing problems.

Although I enjoy my current job, which I've held for three years, I am always interested in exploring new challenges in auto sales. The job of assistant manager at your dealership would be a welcome challenge, and I think my background would make me an asset to your sales team.

My resume is enclosed for your review. I appreciate your consideration and look forward to interviewing with you.

Sincerely,

Terrell Johnson
213/555-9832 (Home)
213/555-2121 (Cell)

ADILA HUSAK
12677 Telegraph Road
Dearborn, MI 48066
A.Husak@xxx.com
(810) 555-2343

April 17, 2005

Robert T. Beatty
Director of Personnel
Turner Broadcasting Co.
One Turner Plaza
Atlanta, GA 33203

Dear Mr. Beatty:

Thank you for taking time today to discuss openings at Turner Broadcasting.
As I mentioned, I am most interested in working for the company in the area
of advertising sales.

Enclosed is the resume you requested. Please note that I have several years of
sales experience, including my time with the Medialink Advertising Agency in
Detroit and KTUT-TV in Auburn Hills. These previous positions have given
me a strong background in media sales. In particular, my employers seem to
appreciate my ability to assess the content and suitability of ads and to analyze
demographic data.

My current goal is to pursue a job in cable television, so I appreciate your
willingness to review my resume and inform me of any suitable opening at
Turner. I will call early next week to discuss whether an interview is in order.

Meanwhile, thank you for your time and encouragement.

Sincerely,

Adila Husak

GLORIA GARLAND

1220 Market Street, #3
San Francisco, CA 92290
415-555-5508
G.Garland@xxx.com

December 2, 2005

Corlis Fenett, Jr.
President
Venture Publishing Corporation
8671 Main Street, Suite 379
New Orleans, LA 70125

Dear Mr. Fenett:

As regional marketing manager of *Bay* Magazine, I have faced many challenges and have handled each of them thoroughly, responsibly, and efficiently. I have learned from and contributed a great deal to the magazine. In this position, I oversee all sales and marketing efforts and the hiring and training of sales staff. I have led the magazine's eastern edition through a difficult reorganization period and planned and implemented new marketing strategies, including new editions for the South.

I have enjoyed my tenure at *Bay*, but I feel it is time to move on to a new challenge. This challenge, I hope, will be the position of Director of Sales and Marketing at Venture Publishing Corporation.

Please find my resume and salary requirements enclosed. Feel free to contact me via e-mail at G.Garland@xxx.com or by phone at (415) 555-5508 if you would like to discuss my qualifications further. Thank you in advance for your consideration.

Sincerely,

Gloria Garland

JOHN L. RYDER
211 W. Timberline Rd.
Boulder, CO 80301
jryder@xxx.com
(719) 555-9080

April 18, 2004

John Junot
Fidelity Insurance Company
52 Riggings Rd.
Denver, CO 80002

Dear Mr. Junot:

I am responding to your advertisement for the Western Sales Manager, which appeared in the April 15th issue of the *Financial News*. Per your request, I have enclosed my resume and list of references.

After several years working as an agent and an adjustor, I am ready to make the move into a sales management position. My extensive experience in the insurance industry has prepared me well for this next step in my career and I believe that I would benefit the Fidelity Group greatly.

I would enjoy discussing my credentials and your current needs in greater detail. I will call early next week to discuss scheduling an interview.

Cordially,

John L. Ryder

Johanna Esposito
152 S. Feather Dr.
Omaha, NE 73802

February 13, 2004

Dear Ms. Evers:

I was intrigued by your ad in the *Omaha Review* for the Bookstore Management Trainee, and I've enclosed my resume and salary requirements as you requested.

All of my life I've been fascinated by books and bookstores. In college I worked in the student bookstore for four years. My work experience also includes experience as a salesperson for Fern Books and as an assistant sales manager for Crown Books in Omaha.

I would enjoy the challenge of applying my experience at Federated Books. Your current needs and my interests seem to match well.

I will call early next week to discuss arranging an interview. Thank you for your time and consideration.

Sincerely,

Johanna Esposito
401/555-9000 (Day)
401/555-6712 (Evening)

DAVID P. JENKINS

365 Wealthy Street, Apt. 1
Grand Rapids, MI 49505
DP.Jenkins@xxx.com
(616) 555-3472

July 23, 2004

Mr. Jeremy Hitleman
Vice President, Sales and Marketing
Sandoval Industries
500 University Drive
Gary, IN 43561

Dear Mr. Hitleman:

I am writing to you to inquire about the possibility of obtaining a position with Sandoval Industries as a sales/marketing manager.

My special interest in working for your company stems from a desire to expand my experience into the area of engine sales. Your company's recent addition of an engine division brought Sandoval to my attention.

Currently, I serve as regional sales manager to Tribor Industries, where I represent four corporate divisions with sales of up to $3 million annually. Previous to this position, I served as district manager for Tribor.

I believe that my sales experience well qualifies me for a position at Sandoval Industries. I hope that reviewing the enclosed resume will convince you of the same.

Thank you for your consideration. I am available at your convenience if you wish to schedule an interview.

Sincerely,

David P. Jenkins

JERRY MATHEWS JR.
6701 W. Mariposa Ave.
Boise, ID 83209
(919) 555-3402

August 18, 2005

Paul H. Harrison
Vice President of Marketing
Boise Electronic Corporation
4000 N. Agricultural Blvd.
Boise, ID 83203

Dear Mr. Harrison:

Boise Electronic has been enjoying tremendous success and growth over the last few years; your company is rapidly becoming a leader in the home electronics field. I am certain that a key factor in that success is a talented sales staff. I have enclosed my resume because I would like to share my experience and talent with Boise.

I currently have seven years of experience in sales with three different companies. Presently, I am a sales assistant with Codaphone, Inc., a company that sells telephone equipment. My position there involves both sales and servicing accounts. Both clients and my employer relay that they value my customer service, communication, and sales skills— qualities that may be equally valuable to Boise Electronic.

I would like to meet to discuss my qualifications. I will call next week to discuss any current openings you may have. Thank you for your time and consideration.

Sincerely,

Jerry Mathews Jr.

Winona T. Simpson
420 W. Easterly Ave.
Indianapolis, IN 49091

June 23, 2005

Thomas E. Eagletender
Pizza Hut, Inc.
4200 Bolt Avenue
Indianapolis, IN 49091

Dear Mr. Eagletender:

David Porter of your marketing department informed me that you were looking for a new marketing manager for your Midwest office. Therefore, I have enclosed my resume so that I may be considered for this position.

Currently, I am the marketing director for Dark Star Video in Indianapolis. Previous to that I was a marketing representative for Jeron Stereo and a public relations assistant for Kader Advertising.

My accomplishments include developing a successful marketing campaign for Dark Star, implementing marketing strategies to increase sales at less-profitable stores, and designing a training program for store managers and staff.

I would like to meet with you at your earliest convenience to discuss this position further. You can reach me at (317) 555-1212. Thank you for considering my credentials.

Yours truly,

Winona T. Simpson

Jennifer Nguyen

35 Desert Rose Way   Las Vegas, NV 46331   JenniferNguyen@xxx.com
(714) 555-6789

October 9, 2004

Felicia Robertson
Gandy's Fine Jewelry
2300 S. Vermont Ave.
Las Vegas, NV 46333

Dear Ms. Robertson:

James Gooden, who is employed by Gandy's, suggested that I send you
a resume. I would like to be considered for any upcoming sales positions
within your jewelry store. I have always wanted to work for Gandy's
because I believe it to be the best fine jewelry store in Las Vegas.

My experience includes sales positions at Stacey's Jewelers and at Eddy
Gems in Las Vegas. My skills include greeting customers, advising them
on purchases, and designing window displays.

I am available at your convenience if you are interested in scheduling an
interview. Thank you for considering me.

Sincerely,

Jennifer Nguyen

Patrick H. McCoy

1701 N. Hampshire Rd.   **(317) 555-3909**
Fort Wayne, IN 46802   **PatMcCoy@xxx.com**

Steven McDougall
Redding Seacraft
7892 Collins Ave.
Bloomington, IN 47403

Dear Mr. McDougall:

I am forwarding my resume in response to the advertisement for a sales manager placed in the August 18th issue of the *Herald Times.*

As my resume indicates, I have an extensive sales background spanning over 10 years. As an account executive for Newmark Industries, I have handled sales accounts in northeastern Indiana and expanded my customer base by 28 percent in the last two years. Prior to that, I worked as a sales representative for Potisco in Terre Haute and for Honoco Manufacturing in Chicago.

I feel confident that I could do an outstanding job as your new sales manager, and I would welcome the opportunity to discuss the opening in person. I am available at your convenience if you would like to arrange an interview.

Sincerely,

Patrick H. McCoy

Gina Kershaw

5001 Lincoln Drive
Marlton, NJ 08053
gina.kershaw@xxx.com
(609) 555-3893

August 3, 2005

Mr. Howard G. Thielking
Director of Personnel
Best Paper Products
500 East Third Street, Suite 1000
Trenton, NJ 08390

Dear Mr. Thielking:

Are you interested in finding new, more effective ways to motivate your sales staff? If so, I think my resume will interest you.

As district sales manager for Harrison Paper Company in Philadelphia, I have developed valuable skills that well qualify me for a management position in your company. After four years at Harrison, I am ready for a change, but I want to continue working within the paper products industry.

Some of my accomplishments at Harrison include increased sales each year, supervision of seven sales representatives, and extensive market research that led to the establishment of several major new accounts.

I am free to interview at any time. Please let me know if you are hiring in this area. Thank you for your time and consideration.

Cordially,

Gina Kershaw